quick little
Quilts

16 7 2 4 1 4

The
Complete Guide to Making
Miniature and Lap Quilts

JANET WICKELL AND DONNA STIDMAN

THE QUILT DIGEST PRESS

NTC/Contemporary Publishing Group

Library of Congress Cataloging-in-Publication Data

Wickell, Janet.
    Quick Little Quilts: The Complete Guide to Miniature and Lap
Quilts / Janet Wickell and Donna Stidman.
       p.   cm.
    ISBN 0-8442-2659-9
     1. Patchwork—Patterns. 2. Quilting. 3. Appliqué.
  4. Miniature quilts.   I. Stidman, Donna. II. Title.
  TT835.W524   1998
  746.46'041—dc21
                                97-46551
                                   CIP

Acknowledgments

We would like to thank Anne Knudsen and everyone at The Quilt Digest Press for giving us the opportunity to make Quick Little Quilts *a reality and for their patience during what has been a chaotic year for us.*

From Janet

Many thanks are due to my family for their ongoing support and encouragement. A special thank you to my daughter, Carly Wickell, who is responsible for making my fabric stash a bit brighter; to Dale Wickell, who builds whatever we need to get the job done; to our parents, Ernest and Thelma Armstrong, for always being there for us; and to Richard Eslinger, whose support at Minifest meant more to us than he probably realizes.

From Donna

I would like to thank my husband, Bill, for his help and patience as we worked on Quick Little Quilts. *Special thanks to all my family for encouraging me to be involved in this project. I could not have done it without you.*

Editorial and production direction by Anne Knudsen
Art direction by Kim Bartko
Project editing by Gerilee Hundt
Book design by Monica Baziuk
Cover design by Monica Baziuk
Cover photography by Sharon Hoogstraten
Drawings by Kandy Petersen
Photography by Sharon Hoogstraten
Manufacturing direction by Pat Martin

Published by The Quilt Digest Press
A division of NTC/Contemporary Publishing Group, Inc.
4255 West Touhy Avenue, Lincolnwood (Chicago), Illinois 60646-1975 U.S.A.
Printed in Singapore
International Standard Book Number: 0-8442-2659-9
  18   17   16   15   14   13   12   11   10   9   8   7   6   5   4   3   2   1

Quick Little Quilts *is dedicated*

to the memory of

Sue Armstrong Eslinger

and Carol Armstrong Baumgarner,

with warm thoughts headed their way

Which Way Do We Go?

Contents

A Joyous Celebration variation

Materials and Supplies

You will not need everything on this list to make each quilt in *Quick Little Quilts*. Read carefully through the pattern you choose to determine which supplies are most suitable. Over time, you will build a collection of these tools and supplies, and more. There are several brands available of each quilting tool. Ask for the advice of your quilt shop to make sure you are buying the materials and supplies that are right for the type of quilt you wish to make.

Cutting
Rotary cutter, mat, and rulers
Extra rotary blades
Sharp, all-purpose shears
Appliqué scissors with pointed tips
Paper scissors

Marking and Templates
#3 or #4 pencils
White or yellow marking pencils
Chalk or soapstone markers
Template plastic
Freezer paper
Tracing paper or newsprint
Carbon paper and tracing wheel
Awl or ⅛" (3 mm) paper punch

Piecing
Sewing machine and ¼" (0.6 cm) presser foot, if available
Extra machine needles
100 percent cotton fabrics
100 percent cotton threads in light-to-dark shades of gray
Fine seam ripper
Fine straight pins
Iron and ironing board
Hand-sewing needles

Finishing
Thin batting
Brass or stainless steel safety pins
Darning needles for basting
Thimble
Cotton quilting thread
Nylon filament for machine quilting
Walking and darning feet for machine quilting
Hand-sewing needles—sharps and betweens

Miscellaneous
Value filter
Hot iron transfer pen
Graph paper
Beeswax

Walk Around the Block

The Quilts

Before you choose a quilt to make, take time to browse through all of the patterns in Chapter 1. You will notice that many are assembled using similar techniques, so the pattern for one quilt may be helpful in designing or assembling another. With the exception of our dollhouse miniatures—*Little Amish Squares* and *Half Log Cabin*—each pattern provides quilt and block dimensions for two sizes. There is a list of fabric requirements for each component of the quilt, along with a detailed cutting chart and step-by-step directions for making the quilt. A special feature titled "Back to Basics" lists topics covered in Chapters 2 through 11 that are most helpful for assembling that particular pattern. Once you have selected a pattern, read it carefully several times to make sure you know exactly how the quilt is made before you begin.

Blazing Baskets

	Small lap	Large lap
Finished quilt	22⅜″ × 25⅜″	44⅜″ × 50⅜″
	59.5 cm × 67.5 cm	118.1 cm × 134.1 cm
Large basket blocks	3¾″ × 3¾″	7½″ × 7½″
	10 cm × 10 cm	20 cm × 20 cm
Small basket blocks	1⅞″ × 1⅞″	3¾″ × 3¾″
	5 cm × 5 cm	10 cm × 10 cm

In *Blazing Baskets* our blocks are on point and surrounded with setting triangles to form a zigzag layout. Triangles around the center column repeat the fabric used in the outer border. Those around the outer blocks are a deep blue mottled fabric. This combination highlights the zigzag effect. We added reduced-scale basket blocks at the corners.

Back to Basics

Cutting Triangles, see page 113

Setting-In, see page 122

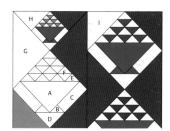

Fabric Requirements *(selvage to selvage)*

	Small lap	Large lap
Baskets		
Body (A) and base (B)	12″ × 12″	¼ yard
	31 cm × 31 cm	0.2 meter
Background (C, D, and E)	¼ yard	½ yard
	0.2 meter	0.5 meter
Flowers, large baskets (F), seven each	2″ × 6″	3″ × 8″
	6 cm × 16 cm	8 cm × 21 cm
Flowers, small baskets (F), four each	2″ × 4″	2″ × 6″
	6 cm × 10 cm	6 cm × 16 cm
Setting Triangles		
Quilt perimeter (G)	15″ × 15″	⅜ yard
	40 cm × 40 cm	0.3 meter

	Small lap	Large lap
Quilt interior (G)	15″ × 15″	⅜ yard × ⅜ yard
	40 cm × 40 cm	*0.3 meter × 0.3 meter*
Small blocks, outer (H)	4″ × 4″	7″ × 7″
	12 cm × 12 cm	*19 cm × 19 cm*
Small blocks, inner (H)	4″ × 4″	7″ × 7″
	12 cm × 12 cm	*19 cm × 19 cm*
Large blocks, corner (I)	4″ × 8″	7″ × 14″
	12 cm × 24 cm	*19 cm × 36 cm*

Borders

	Small lap	Large lap
Inner	2″ × 36″	¼ yard
	6 cm × 90 cm	*0.2 meter*
Outer	⅝ yard	1 yard
	0.5 meter	*0.9 meter*

Finishing

	Small lap	Large lap
Backing	⅞ yard	3 yards, pieced
	0.8 meter	*2.7 meter, pieced*
Batting	29″ × 32″	52″ × 58″
	75 cm × 82 cm	*138 cm × 154 cm*
Binding (running)	110″	202″
	275 cm	*545 cm*

Cutting Chart

		Small lap		Large lap	
Piece	*Description*	*Cut*	*Size*	*Cut*	*Size*

Seven Large Blocks

		Cut	Size	Cut	Size
A	Basket body	4	3⅞″ × 3⅞″	4	6⅞″ × 6⅞″
			10.1 cm × 10.1 cm		*18.1 cm × 18.1 cm*
B	Basket base	7	1⅝″ × 1⅝″	7	2⅜″ × 2⅜″
			4.1 cm × 4.1 cm		*6.1 cm × 6.1 cm*
C	Background, side	14	1¼″ × 2¾″	14	2″ × 5″
			3.2 cm × 7.2 cm		*5.2 cm × 13.2 cm*

Piece	Description	Small lap		Large lap	
		Cut	Size	Cut	Size
D	Background triangle	4	2³⁄₈″ × 2³⁄₈″ 6.1 cm × 6.1 cm	4	3⁷⁄₈″ × 3⁷⁄₈″ 10.1 cm × 10.1 cm
E	Background triangle	14	1⁵⁄₈″ × 1⁵⁄₈″ 4.1 cm × 4.1 cm	14	2³⁄₈″ × 2³⁄₈″ 6.1 cm × 6.1 cm
F*	Half-square triangle units	42	1¼″ 3.2 cm	42	2″ 5.2 cm

*See page 112.

Four Small Blocks

Piece	Description	Small lap		Large lap	
A	Basket body	2	2³⁄₈″ × 2³⁄₈″ 6.1 cm × 6.1 cm	2	3⁷⁄₈″ × 3⁷⁄₈″ 10.1 cm × 10.1 cm
B	Basket base	4	1¼″ × 1¼″ 3.1 cm × 3.1 cm	4	1⁵⁄₈″ × 1⁵⁄₈″ 4.1 cm × 4.1 cm
C	Background, side	8	⁷⁄₈″ × 1⁵⁄₈″ 2.2 cm × 4.2 cm	8	1¼″ × 2³⁄₄″ 3.2 cm × 7.2 cm
D	Block triangle	2	1⁵⁄₈″ × 1⁵⁄₈″ 4.1 cm × 4.1 cm	2	2³⁄₈″ × 2³⁄₈″ 6.1 cm × 6.1 cm
E	Background triangle	8	1¼″ × 1¼″ 3.1 cm × 3.1 cm	8	1⁵⁄₈″ × 1⁵⁄₈″ 4.1 cm × 4.1 cm
F*	Half-square triangle units	24	⁷⁄₈″ 2 cm	24	1¼″ 3 cm

*See page 112.

Setting Triangles

Piece	Description	Small lap		Large lap	
G	Quilt perimeter	2	6³⁄₄″ × 6³⁄₄″ 17.6 cm × 17.6 cm	2	12″ × 12″ 31.6 cm × 31.6 cm
G	Quilt interior	3	6³⁄₄″ × 6³⁄₄″ 17.6 cm × 17.6 cm	3	12″ × 12″ 31.6 cm × 31.6 cm
H	Small blocks, outer	1	4¹⁄₈″ × 4¹⁄₈″ 10.6 cm × 10.6 cm	1	6³⁄₄″ × 6³⁄₄″ 17.6 cm × 17.6 cm
H	Small blocks, inner	1	4¹⁄₈″ × 4¹⁄₈″ 10.6 cm × 10.6 cm	1	6³⁄₄″ × 6³⁄₄″ 17.6 cm × 17.6 cm

Piece	Description	Small lap		Large lap	
		Cut	Size	Cut	Size
I	Large blocks, corner	2	3⅝" × 3⅝" 9.1 cm × 9.1 cm	2	6⅛" × 6⅛" 16.1 cm × 16.1 cm
Borders					
Inner (top and bottom, width)		1	2" 5.2 cm	2	3½" 9.2 cm
Outer (width)*		3	3½" 9.2 cm	4	6½" 16.2 cm

*Cut lengthwise; measure quilt before cutting.

Making the Large Basket Blocks

1. Cut each large A square in half once diagonally.

2. Repeat with each large B, D, and E square.

3. Make six half-square triangle units for each of the seven large baskets (42 total). For a scrappy look, use Method 1 on page 115; for identical half-square triangles use Method 2 on page 115. When ready for block assembly, each half-square triangle unit should measure 1¼" × 1¼" (3.2 cm × 3.2 cm) for the small lap size or 2" × 2" (5.2 cm × 5.2 cm) for the large lap size.

4. Lay out six completed half-square triangle units and four background triangles, E, into four rows. Sew rows.

5. Press seams in adjacent rows in opposite directions. Sew rows together, aligning unit. Match seam intersections carefully. Press new seams toward the darker fabric.

...... ✄ Accuracy Check, page 7

6. Place the flower unit and the large A triangle right sides together, aligning edges carefully. Pin to keep pieces from shifting. Sew together along the longest edge. Press seam toward A triangle.

7. To make a side unit, join a short edge of a large B triangle to a short edge of a large C rectangle. Make another side unit that is a mirror image of the first. Press seams toward the darker fabric. fig.

8. Sew side units to the block. Press seams toward basket. fig. 6

9. Complete the block by adding a large D background triangle. Press seam toward the background triangle. fig. 7

10. Press the block. Use a rotary ruler to verify that it is exactly 4¼″ × 4¼″ (11.2 cm × 11.2 cm) for the small lap or 8″ × 8″ (21.2 cm × 21.2 cm) for the large lap. If the block is too small or slightly skewed, try one of the methods described on page 100 to square it up.

11. Make six more large basket blocks.

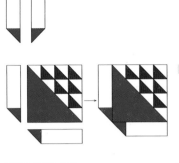

Making the Small Basket Blocks

12. Cut the large A, B, D, and E pieces in half once diagonally, as in Steps 1 and 2 above.

13. Make six half-square triangle units for each of the four small baskets (24 total), as in Step 3 above. Each half-square triangle unit should measure exactly ⅞″ × ⅞″ (2.2 cm × 2.2 cm) for the small lap size or 1¼″ × 1¼″ (3.2 cm × 3.2 cm) for the large lap size.

14. Assemble the block as in Steps 4 to 10 above. If seam allowances are too bulky, trim them back slightly, leaving at least ⅛″ (0.3 cm).

15. Make three more small basket blocks.

Making the Setting Triangles

Because of the zigzag set and the small blocks at the corners, this quilt requires three different sizes of setting triangles. They are all cut by dividing large squares of fabrics. Just how they are divided depends upon their placement in the quilt. Always keep in mind that your goal is to

Accuracy Check

Examine the flower unit you have just assembled. It should be a right-angle triangle measuring 3⅞″ (10.1 cm) for the small lap size or 6⅞″ (18.1 cm) for the large lap size along each of its short legs. Compare the unit to A, the basket base triangle it will be sewn to; their sizes should match. If your flower unit is smaller than it should be or if it is skewed, press it again to make sure bits of width are not hidden in seam allowances. If pressing does not help, examine the unit to find the problem. See pages 100 and 120 for help.

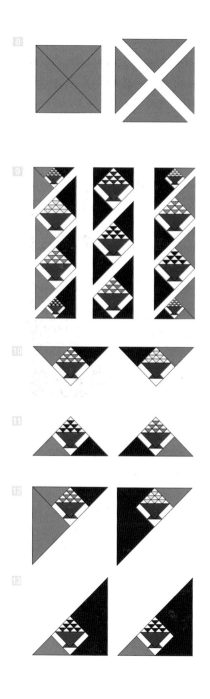

assemble a block or quilt top with straight-grain pieces along outer edges.

16. Cut each G square in half twice diagonally to make four triangles with the straight grain along the longest edge. You will have two extra triangles of each color. Repeat with each H square. fig. 8

17. Cut each I square once diagonally to make two triangles with the straight grain on the shortest edge.

Assembling the Quilt Top

18. Use a design wall or other flat surface to arrange your blocks and setting triangles. If using scrappy blocks, it is helpful to leave the room for a while and then return later for a fresh look. When you are satisfied with the layout, units can be sewn together. fig. 9

19. Sew two contrasting H triangles to the upper sides of an upper small basket block. Press seam allowances toward the triangles. Repeat with the remaining upper small basket, but switch triangles to produce a mirror image of the first unit. fig. 10

20. Sew two contrasting H triangles to the lower sides of a lower small basket block. Press seam allowances toward the triangles. Repeat with the remaining lower small basket, but switch triangles to produce a mirror image of the first unit. fig. 11

21. Sew an outer G setting triangle to the lower left edge of a basket unit assembled in Step 19. Press seam allowance toward the large triangle. Repeat with the remaining basket unit, but use an inner setting triangle. fig. 12

22. Sew an inner G setting triangle to the upper right edge of a basket unit from Step 20. Press seam allowance toward the large triangle. Repeat with the other basket, using outer setting triangle. fig. 13

23. Sew G setting triangles to opposite sides of five large basket blocks. Refer to Figure 9 to see which basket blocks make up these units.

Press seam allowances toward the setting triangles. Place each unit back in the layout. fig. 14

24. Center and sew two I corner triangles to the upper sides of top center basket and two more to the lower side of lower center basket. Press seam allowances toward corner triangles. fig. 15

    ✂ *Accuracy Check*

25. Sew an inner G setting triangle to the lower left edge of the top basket unit. Press seam allowance toward the large triangle. fig. 16

26. Sew an inner G setting triangle to the upper right edge of bottom basket unit. Press seam allowance toward large triangle. fig. 17

Finishing the Quilt

27. Using Figure 9, pin and sew the units together diagonally to form three columns. Seam allowances in adjoining units are pressed in opposite directions, so they should butt against each other to help you match intersections. Sew the three columns together.

28. Cut and add borders (see page 150). The small lap quilt photographed has an inner border along the top and bottom edges only. If you prefer to make a square quilt, omit it or sew a border of equal width to each side before adding the outer border. Both borders are straight sewn.

29. Mark the top for quilting. In the quilt photographed, straight lines were quilted in-the-ditch, and curved lines in borders were meander-quilted, so no marks were necessary.

30. To sandwich, quilt, and bind, see page 155.

Accuracy Check

To determine the midpoint of a triangle's longest edge, fold it in half and crease as you did to assemble blocks. Alternatively, trim the excess seam allowance from the tips of triangles. See Nubbing Triangle Tips on page 122 for help.

A Joyous Celebration

	Miniature	Small lap
Finished quilt	14¾″ × 14¾″	29½″ × 29½″
	38.2 cm × 38.2 cm	74.2 cm × 74.2 cm
Evening Star blocks	2″ × 2″	4″ × 4″
	5.2 cm × 5.2 cm	10 cm × 10 cm
Snowball blocks	2″ × 2″	4″ × 4″
	5.2 cm × 5.2 cm	10 cm × 10 cm

Speed-piecing techniques make stitching this little quilt a breeze. The light fabric that surrounds our Evening Stars blends with the fabric used in the center of Snowball blocks, giving the Snowballs an on-point appearance when the blocks are sewn side by side. If you prefer to work with smaller blocks, try the miniature variation. It is assembled in exactly the same way as the small lap quilt.

Back to Basics

Basics of Patchwork Shapes, see page III
Strip-Piecing Basics, see page 127

Fabric Requirements *(selvage to selvage)*

	Miniature	Lap
Star Blocks		
Points	⅛ yard	¼ yard
	0.1 meter	0.2 meter
Centers	⅛ yard	⅛ yard
	0.1 meter	0.1 meter
Background	⅛ yard	¼ yard
	0.1 meter	0.2 meter
Snowball Blocks		
Centers	⅛ yard	⅜ yard
	0.1 meter	0.3 meter

	Miniature	Lap
Tips	⅛ yard	⅛ yard
	0.1 meter	0.1 meter

Borders

	Miniature	Lap
Inner	⅛ yard	⅛ yard
	0.1 meter	0.1 meter
Outer	¼ yard	⅝ yard
	0.2 meter	0.5 meter

Finishing

	Miniature	Lap
Backing	⅝ yard	1 yard
	0.5 meter	0.9 meter
Batting	19″ × 19″	34″ × 34″
	49 cm × 49 cm	86 cm × 86 cm
Binding (running)	72″	130″
	183 cm	330 cm

Cutting Chart

Description	Miniature		Small lap	
	Cut	Size	Cut	Size
13 Star Blocks				
Star centers	13	1½″ × 1½″	13	2½″ × 2½″
		3.8 cm × 3.8 cm		6.2 cm × 6.2 cm
Background, corners	52	1″ × 1″	52	1½″ × 1½″
		2.5 cm × 2.5 cm		3.8 cm × 3.8 cm
Half-square triangle units*	104	1″	104	1½″
		2.5 cm		3.8 cm

*Use 1⅜″ (3.4 cm) grid for miniature or 1⅞″ (4.6 cm) grid for lap. See page 112.

Description	Miniature		Small lap	
12 Snowball Blocks				
Snowball centers	12	2½″ × 2½″	12	4½″ × 4½″
		6.2 cm × 6.2 cm		11.2 cm × 11.2 cm

Description	Miniature		Small lap	
	Cut	Size	Cut	Size
Snowball corners	48	1" × 1"	48	1½" × 1½"
		2.5 cm × 2.5 cm		3.8 cm × 3.8 cm
Straight-Sewn Borders				
Inner	2	1" strips	4	1½" strips
		2.5 cm		3.8 cm
Outer	2	2" strips	4	4" strips
		5 cm		10 cm

Miniature Tips

· *Use a slightly larger than necessary grid size for half-size triangles, then cut each unit back to exactly 1" (2.5 cm) for the lap quilt or 1½" (3.8 cm) for the miniature before assembling the quilt.*

· *If seam allowances are too bulky, trim back, leaving approximately ³/₁₆" (0.5 cm).*

Making the Star Blocks

1. Make eight half-square triangle units for each of the thirteen Star baskets (104 total). For a scrappy look, use Method 1 on page 115; for identical half-square triangles use Method 2 on page 115. Use a 1⅜" (3.4 cm) grid for the lap quilt or a 1⅞" (4.6 cm) grid for the miniature. Use larger grids if you prefer to sew and cut back for accuracy. Press the seam allowances in half of the units toward the dark fabric and half toward the light fabric.

   ⸺✂ Miniature Tips

2. Match a half-square triangle unit with the seam pressed toward the dark fabric with one in which the seam is pressed toward the light fabric. Sew together. Opposing seams should butt into each other to help achieve a perfect match. Press the new seam allowance to one side. Repeat with all remaining half-square triangle units to make 52 rectangular units. fig.

3. Position four rectangular units, four block corners, and one Star center into three rows. Sew each row together, matching edges carefully. Press seams away from the rectangular units. fig.

4. Sew the rows together, taking care to match edges and seam intersections. Press the block. fig. 3

5. Repeat Steps 3 and 4 to make a total of thirteen Star blocks.

Making the Snowball Blocks

6. Draw a diagonal line from corner to corner on the reverse side of each Snowball corner. The lines will remain in the quilt, so be sure to use a marker that will not bleed with dampness. Pencil, chalk, or permanent marker are good choices. fig. 4

7. Align a marked corner square with a Snowball center, right sides together and matching edges. fig. 5

8. Sew the two together along the marked diagonal line. Trim away excess fabric at the corner, leaving an approximate ¼″ (0.6 cm) seam allowance. fig. 6

9. Repeat, sewing a square to the remaining three corners. Press corners outward to produce the Snowball block. Press carefully to avoid stretching the edges. fig. 7

10. Repeat Steps 7 to 9 to make a total of 12 Snowball blocks.

Assembling the Quilt Top

11. Lay out the quilt by alternating Star and Snowball blocks, placing them in five rows. fig. B

12. Sew the blocks in each row together, matching seam intersections carefully. The V between each set of Star points should intersect and become a continuation of the diagonal seam in adjacent Snowball blocks, making the Snowballs appear to be set on-point. Press seams toward the Snowball blocks.

13. Sew rows together, butting seams and matching all intersections carefully. Press the quilt top.

14. Cut and add borders (see page 145). In the quilt photographed, straight sewn borders were cut on the crosswise grain of the fabric.

Finishing the Quilt

15. Mark the top for quilting.

16. To sandwich, quilt, and bind, see page 155.

Stretching to the Stars

	Miniature	Lap
Finished quilt	20½" × 20½"	40½" × 40½"
	51.2 cm × 51.2 cm	101.2 cm × 101.2 cm
Large Star blocks	4" × 4"	8" × 8"
	10 cm × 10 cm	20 cm × 20 cm
Small Star blocks	2" × 2"	4" × 4"
	5 cm × 5 cm	10 cm × 10 cm

The Stretched Star block illustrates one more layout variation for the versatile half-square triangle unit. No matter which size you choose, quick piecing will help you assemble this quilt easily and in record time. Look at the photograph on page 130 for ideas on altering our layout to suit your needs.

Back to Basics

Basics of Patchwork Shapes, see page III
Strip-Piecing Basics, see page 127

Fabric Requirements *(selvage to selvage)*

	Miniature	Lap
Stars		
Large Star points, nine each print	2" × 6"	3" × 9"
	5 cm × 15 cm	7.6 cm × 23 cm
Small Star points, 16 each print	1¾" × 5"	2" × 6"
	4.4 cm × 2.7 cm	5 cm × 15 cm
Background	⅝ yard	1⅛ yard
	0.5 meter	1 meter
Pieced sashing, inner	⅛ yard	⅜ yard
	0.1 meter	0.3 meter
Pieced sashing, outer	⅛ yard	½ yard
	0.1 meter	0.4 meter

(table continued)

	Miniature	Lap

Finishing

	Miniature	Lap
Backing	28″ × 28″ *71 cm × 71 cm*	2⅔ yards *2.4 meter*
Batting	28″ × 28″ *71 cm × 71 cm*	48″ × 48″ *122 cm × 122 cm*
Binding (running)	95″ *241 cm*	175″ *445 cm*

Cutting Chart

Description	Miniature Cut	Size	Lap Cut	Size

Nine Large Star Blocks

Description	Cut	Size	Cut	Size
Background, rectangles	18	1½″ × 2½″ *3.7 cm × 6.2 cm*	18	2½″ × 4½″ *6.2 cm × 11.2 cm*
Background, squares	54	1½″ × 1½″ *3.7 cm × 3.7 cm*	54	2½″ × 2½″ *6.2 cm × 6.2 cm*
Half-square triangle units:				
Background	27	1⅞″ × 1⅞″ *4.4 cm × 4.4 cm*	27	2⅞″ × 2⅞″ *7.1 cm × 7.1 cm*
Star points	27	1⅞″ × 1⅞″ *4.4 cm × 4.4 cm*	27	2⅞″ × 2⅞″ *7.1 cm × 7.1 cm*

16 Small Star Blocks

Description	Cut	Size	Cut	Size
Background, rectangles	32	1″ × 1½″ *2.5 cm × 3.7 cm*	32	1½″ × 2½″ *3.7 cm × 6.2 cm*
Background, squares	96	1″ × 1″ *2.5 cm × 2.5 cm*	96	1½″ × 1½″ *3.7 cm × 3.7 cm*
Half-square triangle units:				
Background	48	1⅜″ × 1⅜″ *3.4 cm × 3.4 cm*	48	1⅞″ × 1⅞″ *4.6 cm × 4.6 cm*

(table continued)

Description	Miniature Cut	Size	Lap Cut	Size
Star points	48	1⅜" × 1⅜" 3.4 cm × 3.4 cm	48	1⅞" × 1⅞" 4.6 cm × 4.6 cm
Pieced Sashing Strips				
Inner sashing strips	2	1½" × 32" 3.7 cm × 81 cm	5	2½" × 44" 6.2 cm × 112 cm
Outer sashing strips	4	1" × 32" 2.5 cm × 81 cm	10	1½" × 44" 3.7 cm × 112 cm

Making the Large Star Blocks

1. Make six half-square triangle units for each of the nine large Stars (54 total). For a scrappy look, use Method 1 on page 115; for identical half-square triangles use Method 2 on page 115, but use larger pieces of fabric than the scrap sizes given in the fabric requirements chart. When ready for assembly, each half-square triangle unit should measure 1½" × 1½" (3.7 cm × 3.7 cm) for the miniature or 2½" × 2½" (6.2 cm × 6.2 cm) for the lap. Use larger squares if you prefer to sew and cut back for accuracy.

2. Lay out a background rectangle, three background squares, and three half-square triangle units in four rows. Sew them together in rows. Press the seam allowances toward the background pieces. fig. 1

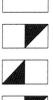

3. Matching seam intersections carefully, sew the four rows together. Press new seam allowances in one direction. fig. 2

4. Repeat Steps 2 and 3 to make a second identical unit.

5. Turn one of the units around and join the two. Be sure to match seams carefully. Press the center seam allowance to one side. fig. 3

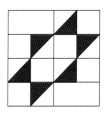

6. Repeat Steps 2 to 5 to make a total of nine large Star blocks.

Making the Small Star Blocks

7. Repeat Step 1 to make six half-square triangle units for each of the sixteen small Stars (96 total). Use square sizes shown in cutting chart. Each completed unit should measure 1″ × 1″ (2.5 cm × 2.5 cm) for the miniature or 1½″ × 1½″ (3.7 cm × 3.7 cm) for the lap quilt.

8. Follow Steps 2 to 5 to make a total of 16 small Star blocks.

Assembling the Quilt Top

9. Sew an outer sashing strip lengthwise to one side of an inner sashing strip. Sew a second outer strip to the opposite side to make a strip set as shown. Press seam allowances toward the center strip. fig.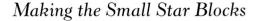

10. Use rotary-cutting equipment to square up one end of the strip set, and then cut 4½″ (11.2 cm) segments for the miniature or 8½″ (21.2 cm) segments for the lap quilt. fig.

11. Assemble and cut additional strip sets to make a total of 24 pieced sashing units.

12. Using a design wall or other flat surface, lay out blocks and sashing segments in seven rows. The quilt photographed on page 16 is an example of a scrappy quilt. Look at the photograph to see how we have arranged the Stars. If you are making a scrappy quilt, you might want to take some time to arrange and rearrange Star blocks until

you are satisfied with the layout. Is it pleasing to you? Leave the room for a while if possible, then return later for a fresh look at the quilt. Does it still please you? If not, reposition the Stars until you are happy with the overall appearance of the quilt top. Sew each row of blocks and sashing together. Press seam allowances toward the sashing. fig. 6

13. Sew the rows together, matching seams carefully.

Finishing the Quilt

14. Mark the top for quilting.

15. To sandwich, quilt, and bind, see page 155.

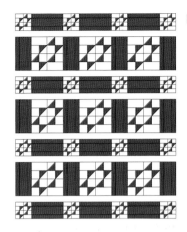

Little Oddfellows Star

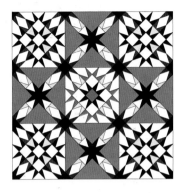

	Small miniature	Miniature
Finished quilt	12½" × 12½"	20½" × 20½"
	31.7 cm × 31.7 cm	*52 cm × 52 cm*
Block	2½" × 2½"	4" × 4"
	6.4 cm × 6.4 cm	*10.2 cm × 10.2 cm*

This little quilt is assembled with two variations of the Oddfellows Star block. The pieced diagonals of both blocks are the same, but one has setting triangles sewn between diagonal elements, while the other contains additional pieced units that add another row to the star tips. The quilt is foundation-pieced, which helps even quilters with little experience sew accurate blocks. The cutting chart may seem intimidating at first, because there appear to be so many pieces, but many are the same sizes and units are pieced in a similar manner.

Back to Basics

Foundation-Piecing Basics, see page 131

Basics of Patchwork Shapes, see page 111

Fabric Basics, see page 95

Fabric Requirements *(selvage to selvage)*

	Small miniature	Miniature
Blocks One and Two		
Light	¼ yard	¼ yard
	0.2 meter	*0.2 meter*
Medium-light	⅛ yard	¼ yard
	0.1 meter	*0.2 meter*
Medium-dark	⅛ yard	¼ yard
	0.1 meter	*0.2 meter*
Dark	¼ yard	¼ yard
	0.2 meter	*0.2 meter*

(table continued)

	Small miniature	Miniature
Borders		
Light inner border, scrap	¾" × 33" 1.9 cm × 84 cm	2" × 44" 5 cm × 112 cm
Dark outer border	¼ yard 0.2 meter	½ yard 0.4 meter
Finishing		
Backing	½ yard 0.4 meter	¾ yard 0.6 meter
Batting	17" × 17" 43 cm × 43 cm	25" × 25" 64 cm × 64 cm
Binding (running)	65" 165 cm	95" 241 cm

Cutting Chart

		Small miniature		Miniature
Piece	Fabric	Cut	Size	Size

Variation One Blocks

Use Foundation A for the small miniature or E for the miniature. Make four.

Piece	Fabric	Cut	Size	Size
1	Light	4	1" × 1½" 2.5 cm × 3.8 cm	1¼" × 1¾" 3.2 cm × 4.4 cm
2, 3	Medium-dark	4	1" × 2" 2.5 cm × 5 cm	1¼" × 2¼" 3.2 cm × 5.7 cm
4	Dark	2	1" × 1" 2.5 cm × 2.5 cm	1¾" × 1¾" 4.4 cm × 4.4 cm
5, 6	Medium-dark	4	1" × 2" 2.5 cm × 5 cm	1¼" × 2¼" 3.2 cm × 5.7 cm
7	Light	4	1" × 1" 2.5 cm × 2.5 cm	1½" × 1½" 3.8 cm × 3.8 cm
8, 9	Dark	4	1" × 2" 2.5 cm × 5 cm	1¼" × 2¼" 3.2 cm × 5.7 cm

(table continued)

Foundation Templates

Foundation Templates A, B, C, D, E, F, G,
and H are provided on page 173.

Variation One

Piece	Fabric	Cut	Small miniature Size	Miniature Size
10	Medium-dark	4	1″ × 1″ 2.5 cm × 2.5 cm	1½″ × 1½″ 3.8 cm × 3.8 cm

Use Foundation B for the small miniature or F for the miniature. Make 12.

Piece	Fabric	Cut	Size	Size
1	Light	12	1″ × 1½″ 2.5 cm × 3.8 cm	1¼″ × 1¾″ 3.2 cm × 4.4 cm
2, 3	Medium-dark	12	1″ × 2″ 2.5 cm × 5 cm	1¼″ × 2¼″ 3.2 cm × 5.7 cm
4	Dark	6	1″ × 1″ 2.5 cm × 2.5 cm	1¾″ × 1¾″ 4.4 cm × 4.4 cm
5, 6	Medium-light	12	1″ × 2″ 2.5 cm × 5 cm	1¼″ × 2¼″ 3.2 cm × 5.7 cm
7	Light	12	1″ × 1″ 2.5 cm × 2.5 cm	1½″ × 1½″ 3.8 cm × 3.8 cm
8, 9	Dark	12	1″ × 2″ 2.5 cm × 5 cm	1¼″ × 2¼″ 3.2 cm × 5.7 cm

Large side triangles

Piece	Fabric	Cut	Size	Size
	Dark	2	3⅛″ × 3⅛″ 7.9 cm × 7.9 cm	4¼″ × 4¼″ 10.8 cm × 10.8 cm

Variation Two Blocks

Use Foundation A for the small miniature or E for the miniature. Make five.

Piece	Fabric	Cut	Size	Size
1	Light	5	1″ × 1½″ 2.5 cm × 3.8 cm	1¼″ × 1¾″ 3.2 cm × 4.4 cm
2, 3	Medium-dark	5	1″ × 2″ 2.5 cm × 5 cm	1¼″ × 2¼″ 3.2 cm × 5.7 cm
4	Dark	3	1″ × 1″ 2.5 cm × 2.5 cm	1¾″ × 1¾″ 4.4 cm × 4.4 cm
5, 6	Medium-light	5	1″ × 2″ 2.5 cm × 5 cm	1¼″ × 2¼″ 3.2 cm × 5.7 cm
7	Light	5	1″ × 1″ 2.5 cm × 2.5 cm	1½″ × 1½″ 3.8 cm × 3.8 cm

Variation Two

Piece	Fabric	Cut	Small miniature Size	Miniature Size
8, 9	Dark	5	1″ × 2″ 2.5 cm × 5 cm	1¼″ × 2¼″ 3.2 cm × 5.7 cm
10	Medium-dark	5	1″ × 1″ 2.5 cm × 2.5 cm	1½″ × 1½″ 3.8 cm × 3.8 cm

Use Foundation B for the small miniature or F for the miniature. Make 15.

Piece	Fabric	Cut	Small miniature Size	Miniature Size
1	Light	15	1″ × 1½″ 2.5 cm × 3.8 cm	1¼″ × 1¾″ 3.2 cm × 4.4 cm
2, 3	Medium-light	15	1″ × 2″ 2.5 cm × 5 cm	1¼″ × 2¼″ 3.2 cm × 5.7 cm
4	Dark	8	1″ × 1″ 2.5 cm × 2.5 cm	1¾″ × 1¾″ 4.4 cm × 4.4 cm
5, 6	Medium-light	15	1″ × 2″ 2.5 cm × 5 cm	1¼″ × 2¼″ 3.2 cm × 5.7 cm
7	Light	15	1″ × 1″ 2.5 cm × 2.5 cm	1½″ × 1½″ 3.8 cm × 3.8 cm
8, 9	Dark	15	1″ × 2″ 2.5 cm × 5 cm	1¼″ × 2¼″ 3.2 cm × 5.7 cm

Use Foundation C for the small miniature or G for the miniature. Make 20.

Piece	Fabric	Cut	Small miniature Size	Miniature Size
1	Light	20	1″ × 1½″ 2.5 cm × 3.8 cm	1½″ × 1¾″ 3.8 cm × 4.4 cm
2, 3	Dark	20	1″ × 2″ 2.5 cm × 5 cm	1¼″ × 2¼″ 3.2 cm × 5.7 cm
4	Light	20	2″ × 2″ 5 cm × 5 cm	2½″ × 2½″ 6.4 cm × 6.4 cm

Use Foundation D for the small miniature or H for the miniature. Make 20.

Piece	Fabric	Cut	Small miniature Size	Miniature Size
1	Light	20	1″ × 1½″ 2.5 cm × 3.8 cm	1½″ × 1¾″ 3.8 cm × 4.4 cm
2, 3	Dark	20	1″ × 2″ 2.5 cm × 5 cm	1¼″ × 2¼″ 3.2 cm × 5.7 cm

(table continued)

| Piece | Fabric | Small miniature | | Miniature |
		Cut	Size	Size
4	Light	20	2" × 2" 5 cm × 5 cm	2½" × 2½" 6.4 cm × 6.4 cm

Inner Border

| | Light | 1 | ¾" × 33"
1.9 cm × 84 cm | 2   1" × 44"
2.5 cm × 112 cm |
| | Dark | 2 | 2½" × 44"
6.4 cm × 112 cm | 3   4" × 44"
10 cm × 112 cm |

Sewing Tip

For quicker sewing, mark desired fabric arrangement on a master block, or directly on each foundation.

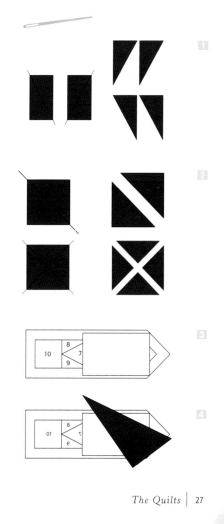

Making Variation One Blocks

Foundation A or E

1. Using Foundation A for the small miniature or Foundation E for the miniature, cut rectangles for Pieces 2 and 3, 5 and 6, and 8 and 9 in half once diagonally. Cut half along one diagonal, and cut the rest along the opposite diagonal to make mirror-image triangles. fig. 1

2. Cut squares for Piece 4 in half once diagonally. Cut large squares for large side triangles in half twice diagonally. fig. 2

3. Position a Piece 1 rectangle right side up on the reverse (unprinted) of a foundation. Secure with a pin or glue stick. Hold the foundation up to the light, printed side facing you. Make sure the edges of the rectangle overlap all lines for Piece 1 and that the overlap creates a stable seam allowance when they are sewn. fig. 3

   ✂ *Sewing Tip*

4. Position a Piece 2 triangle right side down on the rectangle, aligning its diagonal edge to overlap the printed line separating Pieces 1 and 2. If you're in doubt about which triangle type to use, lay it right side up over Piece 2 on the reverse of the foundation to make sure its shape matches. Flip it over for alignment. fig. 4

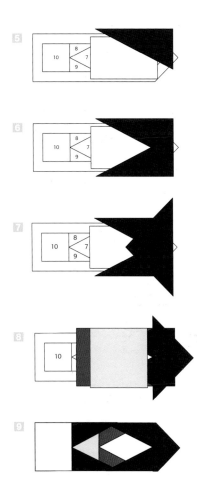

5. Holding fabrics in place, turn the foundation over and sew on the line separating Piece 1 from Piece 2, starting and stopping a few stitches on either side. Remove from machine and flip Piece 2 right side up. Check to make sure its edges overlap all surrounding seam lines. Trim seam allowance to reduce bulk and press. fig. 5

✁ Foundation-Piecing Tips, page 29

6. Position Piece 3 right side down on Piece 1. Sew to foundation as above. Verify placement and trim the seam allowance. fig. 6

7. Center a Piece 4 triangle right side down across the tops of Pieces 2 and 3. The triangle's long edge should overlap the point of Piece 1 by ¼" (0.6 cm). Sew Piece 4 to the foundation. Verify placement and trim all layers of seam allowance. Flip upright. fig. 7

8. Sew Pieces 5 and 6 to the foundation in the same manner.

9. Center an edge of Piece 7 right side down on the foundation, using the tip of Piece 1 as a reference for correct placement. Sew, check, and trim seams. Flip upright. fig. 8

10. Sew Pieces 8 and 9 to the foundation in the same manner as for other long triangles.

11. Sew Piece 10 to the foundation in the same manner as Piece 7. Use the tip of Piece 7 as a guide to placement.

12. Press the foundation. Trim all layers on the outer edge of the outer-most line of the foundation. fig. 9

13. Repeat to make a total of four A or E units.

Foundation B (Small Miniature) or F (Miniature)

14. Using Foundation B for the small miniature or Foundation F for the miniature, make 12 foundation units. They are assembled as previous units but without Piece 10. fig. 10

15. Sew a B unit to the square end of an A unit, or an E unit to an F unit. Remove paper and press toward center. fig. 11

16. Sew a short side of a large corner triangle to each of the remaining units. Match carefully and use the seam line on the template to sew exact ¼″ (0.6 cm) seams. Remove paper and press toward large triangles. Repeat to make another identical unit. fig. 12

17. Sew a unit from Step 16 to each side of the long unit from Step 15, matching ends and center seam intersections carefully. Remove papers from seam allowances only and press block. fig. 13

18. Follow Steps 15 through 17 to make three more identical blocks.

Making Variation Two Blocks

Foundation A (Small Miniature) or E (Miniature)

19. Using Foundation A for the small miniature or E for the miniature and following Steps 1 to 13, sew five foundation units. Using Foundation B for the small miniature or F for the miniature, sew 15 units.

20. Using Foundation C for the small miniature or G for the miniature, cut Piece 2 and 3 rectangles in half once diagonally as before. Cut half in one direction, and cut remaining rectangles along the opposite diagonal.

21. Cut Piece 4 triangles in half twice diagonally as you did large side triangles for block Variation One.

22. Place a Piece 1 rectangle right side up on reverse of template. fig. 14

23. Sew Piece 2 and 3 triangles to the template in the same manner as previous long triangles. fig. 15

24. Position a Piece 4 triangle right side down on the reverse of the template. A short edge should overlap the line between Pieces 3 and

Foundation-Piecing Tips

Make a sample of each block variation before cutting all patches for the quilt. Our patch sizes are generous and allow for variation in placement. After you are comfortable with the technique you may be able to reduce sizes.

· *Check patch placement after every addition. Patches must extend beyond seam lines, and outermost patches must extend slightly past the outer edge of the foundation.*

· *Trim seams in the small miniature to approximately ⅛″ (0.3 cm), and use a slightly smaller stitch length to help strengthen seams.*

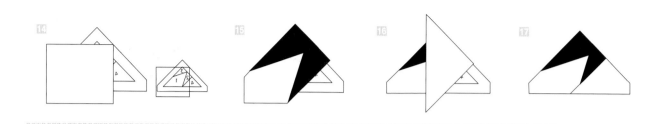

4 by approximately ¼″ (0.6 cm). Sew on the line and check placement before trimming seam and pressing in place. fig. 16

25. Press the block and trim on the outer edge of the outermost line. fig. 17

26. Repeat Steps 22 through 25 to assemble a total of 20 identical units.

27. Using Foundation D for the small miniature or H for the miniature, cut Piece 2 and 3 rectangles in half diagonally as before.

28. Place a Piece 1 rectangle right side up on reverse foundation. fig. 18

29. Sew Piece 2 and 3 triangles to the foundation as other long triangles.

30. Align a Piece 4 square with the unit, right side down. Use the point of Piece 1 to judge alignment as before. fig. 19

31. Sew Piece 4 to the unit. Verify placement, trim allowance, and flip upright. Press the block. Trim on outer line. fig. 20

32. Repeat Steps 27 through 31 to assemble a total of 20 identical units.

33. Sew a C unit to a D unit for the small miniature or a G unit to an H unit for the miniature. Match edges carefully. The resulting units replace the large inset triangles used in the first block. fig. 21

34. Sew together five A-B (small miniature) or E-F (miniature) pairs as for the first block.

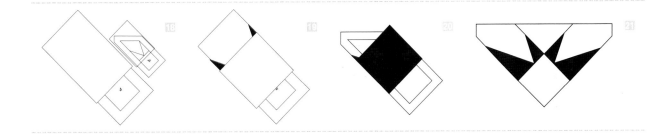

35. Sew a pieced unit from Step 16 to B or F units in the same manner as plain triangles were sewn in the first block. Remove papers from seam allowances and press seams toward the pieced triangles. Repeat for all remaining units.

36. Align a pieced side triangle (C-D for the small miniature or G-H for the miniature) with a narrow diagonal unit (B or F), matching edges and seam intersections. Pin. Sew together. Remove papers from seam allowances only and press the block.

37. Make a total of five identical blocks.

Assembling the Quilt Top

38. Lay out the quilt top by assembling three rows. Each row contains three alternating blocks. Refer to the photograph on page 22.

39. Sew the blocks in each row together, matching edges and seam intersections. Remove paper and press allowances in adjoining rows in opposite directions. Sew rows together.

40. Measure and add borders as described on page 150. Remove all papers.

Finishing the Quilt

41. Mark the top for quilting as desired.

42. To sandwich, quilt, and bind, see page 155.

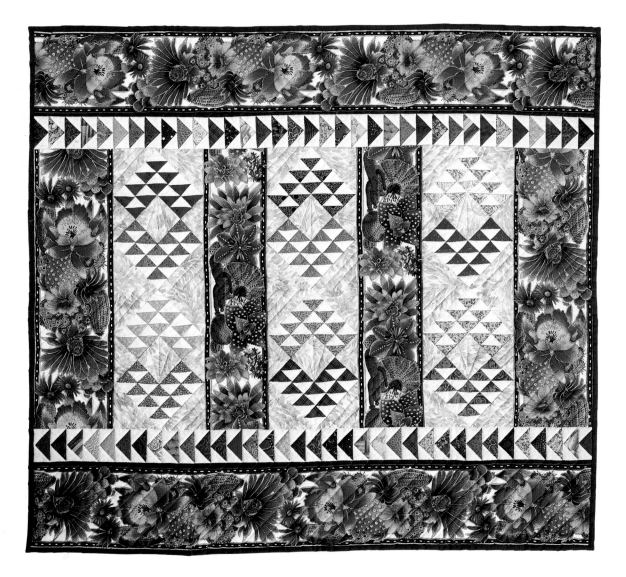

Which Way Do We Go?

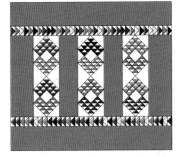

	Miniature	Lap
Finished quilt	23" × 22"	35½" × 31½"
	58.4 cm × 55.8 cm	90.2 cm × 80 cm

This quilt is assembled with quick-pieced half-square triangle units forming traditional Winged Square blocks. Blocks are placed in columns and surrounded by border prints and foundation-pieced Flying Geese.

Fabric Requirements *(selvage to selvage)*

	Miniature	Lap
Background	⅜ yard	½ yard
	0.3 meter	0.4 meter
Blocks and Border		
12 darks	5" × 7"	6" × 9"
	12.7 cm × 17.8 cm	15 cm × 22 cm
Light	⅜ yard	⅝ yard
	0.3 meter	0.5 cm
Border stripe	¾ yard	1⅛ yard*
	0.7 meter	1 meter
Finishing		
Backing	¾ yard	1 yard
	0.7 meter	0.9 meter
Batting	26" × 24"	41" × 37"
	66 cm × 61 cm	104 cm × 94 cm
Binding (running)	100"	150"
	254 cm	380 cm

*See Cutting Chart for strip widths.

(table continued)

Back to Basics

Basics of Patchwork Shapes, see page III
Foundation-Piecing Basics, see page 131

Cutting Chart

Description	Miniature		Lap	
	Cut	Size	Cut	Size

Winged Square Columns

Description	Cut	Size	Cut	Size
Center squares	6	2″ × 2″ 5 cm × 5 cm	6	2½″ × 2½″ 6.4 cm × 6.4 cm
Side triangles	3	3⅜″ × 3⅜″ 8.6 cm × 8.6 cm	3	4⅛″ × 4⅛″ 10.5 cm × 10.5 cm
Setting triangles	2	5½″ × 5½″ 13.9 cm × 13.9 cm	2	7″ × 7″ 17.8 cm × 17.8 cm
Corner triangles	6	3″ × 3″ 7.6 cm × 7.6 cm	6	3¾″ × 3¾″ 9.5 cm × 9.5 cm
Half-square triangle units:				
Dark fabrics, each of 12	6	1⅝″ × 1⅝″ 4.1 cm × 4.1 cm	6	1⅞″ × 1⅞″ 4.7 cm × 4.7 cm
Light fabric	72	1⅝″ × 1⅝″ 4.1 cm × 4.1 cm	72	1⅞″ × 1⅞″ 4.7 cm × 4.7 cm

Border Stripe

Description	Cut	Size	Cut	Size
Inner vertical border	2	2½″ × at least 14″ 6.4 cm × at least 36 cm	2	4½″ × at least 18″ 11.4 cm × at least 46 cm
Outer vertical border	2	3½″ × at least 14″ 8.9 cm × at least 36 cm	2	5½″ × at least 18″ 13.9 cm × at least 46 cm
Outer horizontal border	2	3½″ × at least 25″ 8.9 cm × at least 64 cm	2	5½″ × at least 33″ 13.9 cm × at least 84 cm

Flying Geese Pieced Borders

Description	Cut	Size	Cut	Size
Dark squares, scrappy assortment	30	2″ × 2″ 5 cm × 5 cm	36	2½″ × 2½″ 6.4 cm × 6.4 cm
Light squares	60	1¾″ × 1¾″ 4.4 cm × 4.4 cm	72	2⅛″ × 2⅛″ 5.4 cm × 5.4 cm

Making the Winged Square Blocks

1. Using six light and six dark squares for each, make twelve identical half-square triangle units for each of the twelve half blocks (144 total). For help, see Method 1 on page 115. When ready for block assembly, each half-square triangle unit should measure 1¼″ × 1¼″ (3.2 cm × 3.2 cm) for the miniature or 1½″ × 1½″ (3.8 cm × 3.8 cm) for the lap quilt.

2. To make the small side triangles, cut each of the three background squares in half twice diagonally. fig. 1

3. To make the large setting triangles, cut each of the two large background squares in half twice diagonally.

4. To make the corner triangles, cut each of the six background squares in half once diagonally. fig. 2

5. Arrange two groups of 12 triangle units, one center square, and two small side triangles. Sew together diagonally. Press seam allowances as indicated by arrows. fig. 3

6. Matching seam intersections carefully, sew the diagonal rows together to complete the block. fig. 4

7. Repeat Steps 5 and 6 to make a total of six blocks.

Assembling the Quilt Top

8. Arrange two blocks, two setting triangles, and four corner triangles in a column. Sew two background corner squares to the top and bottom blocks, and sew a large setting triangle to each block. Press allowances toward the background pieces. fig. 5

9. Connect the column along the remaining diagonal, matching seam intersections carefully. Press. fig. 6

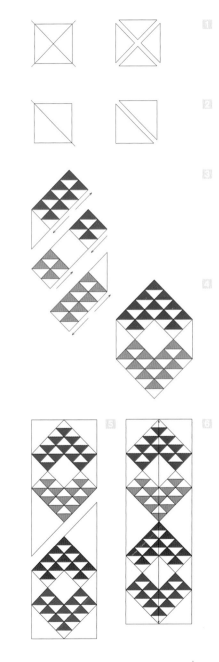

10. Repeat Steps 8 and 9, making two more columns of blocks. Two setting triangles will not be used.

11. Measure each column through its vertical midpoint. Ideally, lengths should be the same. Realistically, they may differ slightly. Select one border length that will be workable with all three. Cut two narrow border print strips and two wide border print strips to match this length.

12. Sew a narrow border to the right side of a block column, matching and pinning midpoints first. Continue matching the border's edge along the entire side of the column, easing in fullness if necessary. Press seam allowance toward the border.

13. Sew another column of blocks to the opposite side of the border.

14. Add the remaining narrow border to the right side of the second column, and then add the third column of blocks.

15. Sew a wide border print to each side of the quilt top, matching as for narrow borders. fig. 7

Making the Flying Geese Pieced Border

16. Measure the quilt through its horizontal midpoint.

17. Deduct ½" (1.2 cm) from the measurement determined in Step 1. Use the remainder to determine how many Flying Geese you need to cross the width of the quilt. For example, our 35½" (90 cm) quilt required 35 1" Flying Geese for each pieced border. The Flying Geese used in the miniature version finish at ¾". Small width differences can be eased in, if necessary.

18. For the small lap quilt, make paper foundations of Template A on page 171. Use Template B for the miniature quilt. For help, see page 133. Our border foundations *do not* include seam allowances.

Transfer the template to paper as many times as necessary, adjusting the lengths to match the exact number of Flying Geese required for each border of your quilt. Before piecing, draw a seam allowance ¼″ (0.6 cm) away from all sides of each foundation.

19. Gather the dark and light border squares. Cut each square in half once diagonally as in Figure 2. Stack the triangles, mixing up the darks for a scrappy effect.

20. Follow the directions on page 135 to foundation piece the geese.

21. Piece all segments required to achieve each border length. Trim each segment on its outermost line, making sure that line includes a ¼″ (0.6 cm) seam allowance. Orient the Flying Geese in the same direction and sew segments together end to end to assemble the borders. Do not remove papers yet.

22. Using the photograph as a guide, pin a Flying Geese border to the top of your quilt, matching ends and midpoints first and then continuing to align the border along the entire width. Sew the border to the quilt. Repeat on the bottom of the quilt.

23. Cut two wide border print strips the exact length determined in Step 16. Match and sew them to the quilt. Remove the paper foundations. Press the quilt top.

Finishing the Quilt

24. Mark the top for quilting.

25. To sandwich, quilt, and bind, see page 155.

Borders

Most border points have well-defined lines on their outer edges, making it easy to make ¼″ (0.6 cm) cuts from each edge to add seam allowances. If you find a border print you love but whose stripes finish at different widths than ours, go ahead and use it. Just keep in mind that the dimensions of your quilt will change and the number of Flying Geese required for the pieced borders will differ. For the miniature, you might consider using just part of a border stripe. Many have vertical divisions, making it easy to eliminate part of the width.

Carolina Byways

	Miniature	Lap
Finished quilt	15½″ × 15½″	30½″ × 30½″
	38.7 cm × 38.7 cm	76.2 cm × 76.2 cm
Nine-Patch blocks	3″ × 3″	6″ × 6″
	7.5 cm × 7.5 cm	15 cm × 15 cm

Most patterns for the Split Nine-Patch block involve cutting and piecing individual squares and triangles. Our method uses strip-piecing techniques. The blocks go together quickly and are always accurate if you take care to cut your strips precisely and use an exact ¼″ (0.6 cm) seam allowance. The quilt shown opposite was sewn with an assortment of contemporary florals that seem to melt into each other, while the quilt on page 126 is arranged in a traditional Barn Raising layout. It is difficult to tell that they were both assembled with the same Split Nine-Patch block.

Back to Basics

Color Value, see page 98

Strip-Piecing Basics, see page 127

Fabric Requirements *(selvage to selvage)*

	Miniature	Lap
Nine-Patch Blocks*		
Darks	½ yard	¾ yard
	0.4 meter	0.6 meter
Medium darks	¼ yard	½ yard
	0.2 meter	0.4 meter
Lights	½ yard	¾ yard
	0.4 meter	0.6 meter
Medium lights	¼ yard	½ yard
	0.2 meter	0.4 meter

*See Cutting Chart.

(table continued)

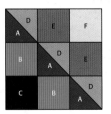

	Miniature	Lap

Finishing

	Miniature	Lap
Backing	⅝ yard *0.5 meter*	1⅛ yards *1 meter*
Batting	19″ × 19″ *48 cm × 48 cm*	35″ × 35″ *88 cm × 88 cm*
Binding (running)	72″ *183 cm*	135″ *343 cm*

Cutting Chart

Piece	Description	Cut	Size for miniature	Size for small lap

Four Split Nine-Patch Blocks*

Dark half blocks (for each half):

Piece	Description	Cut	Size for miniature	Size for small lap
A	Dark strips	2	2″ × 7″ *4.7 cm × 18 cm*	3″ × 11″ *7.2 cm × 28 cm*
A	Dark squares	4	2″ × 2″ *4.7 cm × 4.7 cm*	3″ × 3″ *7.2 cm × 7.2 cm*
B	Medium-dark strips	2	1½″ × 7″ *3.7 cm × 18 cm*	2½″ × 11″ *6.2 cm × 28 cm*
C	Dark strip for outer corner	1	1½″ × 7″ *3.7 cm × 18 cm*	2½″ × 11″ *6.2 cm × 28 cm*

Light half blocks (for each half):

Piece	Description	Cut	Size for miniature	Size for small lap
D	Light strips	2	2″ × 7″ *4.7 cm × 18 cm*	3″ × 11″ *7.2 cm × 28 cm*
D	Light squares	4	2″ × 2″ *4.7 cm × 4.7 cm*	3″ × 3″ *7.2 cm × 7.2 cm*
E	Medium-light strips	2	1½″ × 7″ *3.7 cm × 18 cm*	2½″ × 11″ *6.2 cm × 28 cm*
F	Light strip, outer corner	1	1½″ × 7″ *3.7 cm × 18 cm*	2½″ × 11″ *6.2 cm × 28 cm*

*Cut a total of seven groups of strips.

Making the Dark Block Halves

1. Choose two dark fabrics and one medium-dark fabric. Cut strips the length and width required for the chosen block size, as shown in the Cutting Chart.

2. Sew a dark Fabric A strip lengthwise to a medium-dark Fabric B strip. Sew the dark Fabric C strip to the opposite side of Fabric B to produce a strip set. Press seam allowances toward the C strip. fig. 1

3. Square up one end of the strip set. Cut four segments as shown. For the miniature, the segment length is 1½″ (3.7 cm); for the small lap quilt it is 2½″ (6.2 cm). fig. 2

4. Sew remaining dark Fabric A strip to one side of remaining medium-dark Fabric B strip. Press seam toward darker strip, Fabric A. fig. 3

5. Square up one end of the strip set, and then cut four segments from it, using the same segment length as in Step 3. Set segments aside. fig. 4

6. Position a Step 3 segment, a Step 5 segment and a Fabric A square so that like fabrics form a diagonal. Match seam intersections carefully and sew them together. Press new seam allowances toward the bottom of the block half. fig. 5

7. Repeat Step 6 to make a total of four identical block halves.

8. Using see-through template plastic, cut out a 3⅞″ (9.6 cm) square for the miniature or 6⅞″ (17.1 cm) square for the small lap quilt. Slice the square in half once diagonally. Use the resulting triangles to trim your half blocks. fig. 6

9. Tape one triangle to a rotary-cutting ruler, as shown, carefully aligning its long edge flush with the edge of the ruler. If the template

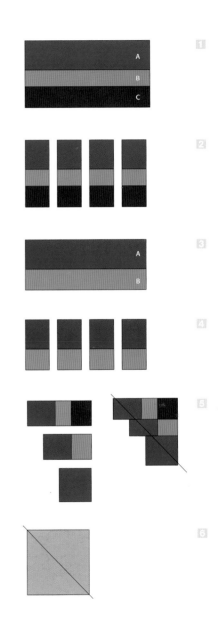

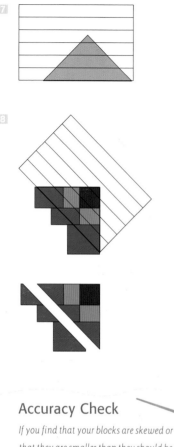

is difficult to see through the ruler, align masking tape along its short edges to make them visible. fig. 7

10. Align the horizontal and vertical sides of the template to the corresponding sides of a half block. Make sure the first ¼" (0.6 cm) line of the ruler passes through the triangle points that run along the diagonal edge. That line indicates where your seam line will be when block halves are connected. Hold the ruler firmly in place and trim the block along the diagonal to make it exactly the same size as the template. Repeat with remaining blocks. fig. 8

11. Select six additional sets of two dark and one medium-dark fabric. Cut and sew pieces for each set in the same manner as the first, making four identical block halves from each grouping (28 total). Your dark block halves are now ready for use.

Making the Light Block Halves

12. Choose two light fabrics and one medium-light fabric for your first light block half. Cut strips as in Step 1.

13. Assemble Fabrics D, E, and F into half blocks as in Steps 2 through 10. fig. 9

14. Choose six additional sets of two light and one medium-light fabric. Cut and sew pieces for each set in the same manner as the first, making four identical block halves from each grouping (28 total). Your light block halves are now ready for use.

Assembling the Quilt Top

15. Align a dark block half and a light block half, right sides together. Carefully match seams where half-square triangles meet along diagonal edge. Use a ¼" (0.6 cm) seam allowance to sew the diagonal

Accuracy Check

If you find that your blocks are skewed or that they are smaller than they should be, try pressing seams in strip sets open. We usually recommend pressing seams to one side for strength, but this is not critical for a quilt that will receive little wear and tear.

seam. For a scrappy look, avoid sewing an entire batch of identical light halves to another batch of identical dark halves.

16. Press seam to one side. Trim nubs created from seam allowance.

17. Lay out blocks for your quilt top. To make a quilt similar to the one photographed, arrange your blocks in five rows of five blocks. You will have three extra blocks to help with design manipulations. fig. 10

18. Sew the blocks in each row together, and then join the rows. Match all seam intersections carefully.

Finishing the Quilt

19. Mark the top for quilting.

20. To sandwich, quilt, and bind, see page 155.

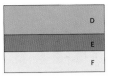

Medallion Star

	Miniature	Wallhanging
Finished quilt	17½″ × 17½″	34½″ × 34½″
	43.2 cm × 43.2 cm	85.2 cm × 85.2 cm
Center Star block	6″ × 6″	12″ × 12″
	15 cm × 15 cm	30 cm × 30 cm
Small Star blocks	3″ × 3″	6″ × 6″
	7.5 cm × 7.5 cm	15 cm × 15 cm

This is probably the most challenging quilt in the book. It will give you lots of practice setting-in patches. Select a border print that you love, and then build your other colors around it. The quilt does not have traditional borders; two different fabrics, cut with templates, were used to frame the blocks. Mirror-image border print strips meet to form a lacy design at mitered corners. The same print was used in the center of our large Star, where identical triangles are joined to form a kaleidoscope-like square. If you have difficulty finding border prints, use any colorful print with a symmetrical, repeating pattern.

Back to Basics

Basics of Patchwork Shapes, see page III

Setting-In, see page 122

Fabric Requirements *(selvage to selvage)*

	Miniature	Wallhanging
Center Star Block		
Center square	Cut from border print fabric	
Tips, dark	4″ × 7″	6″ × 11″
	10 cm × 18 cm	15 cm × 28 cm
Tips, highlight	3¼″ × 3¼″	5¼″ × 5¼″
	8.1 cm × 8.1 cm	13.1 cm × 13.1 cm
Background	6″ × 6″	12″ × 12″
	15 cm × 15 cm	30 cm × 30 cm

	Miniature	Wallhanging
Small Star Blocks		
Centers	4″ × 8″	⅛ yard
	10 cm × 20 cm	0.1 meter
Tips, eight darks	3″ × 5″	4″ × 7″
	7.5 cm × 13 cm	10 cm × 18 cm
Tips, highlight	5″ × 12″	⅛ yard
	13 cm × 30 cm	0.1 meter
Background	⅛ yard	¼ yard
	0.1 meter	0.2 meter
Framing		
Framing fabric and corners	¼ yard	⅜ yard
	0.2 meter	0.3 meter
Borders		
Inner, border print*	¾ yard	1 yard
	0.6 meter	0.9 meter
Outer	¼ yard	⅝ yard
	0.2 meter	0.5 meter

*With 2⅛″ (8.4 cm) finished stripe for miniature or 4¼″ (10.8 cm) finished stripe for wallhanging.

Finishing		
Backing	21″ × 21″	1⅛ yard
	53 cm × 53 cm	1 meter
Batting	21″ × 21″	38″ × 38″
	53 cm × 53 cm	97 cm × 97 cm
Binding (running)	80″	150″
	203 cm	381 cm

(table continued)

Cutting Chart

Description	Miniature		Wallhanging	
	Cut	Size	Cut	Size

Eight Small Star Blocks

Description	Cut	Size	Cut	Size
Star centers	8	1½″ × 1½″ 3.7 cm × 3.7 cm	8	2½″ × 2½″ 6.2 cm × 6.2 cm
Background, corners	32	1½″ × 1½″ 3.7 cm × 3.7 cm	32	2½″ × 2½″ 6.2 cm × 6.2 cm
Star tip units:				
Background	8	2¼″ × 2¼″ 5.6 cm × 5.6 cm	8	3¼″ × 3¼″ 8.1 cm × 8.1 cm
Tips (two per block)	16	2¼″ × 2¼″ 5.6 cm × 5.6 cm	16	3¼″ × 3¼″ 8.1 cm × 8.1 cm
Tips, highlight	8	2¼″ × 2¼″ 5.6 cm × 5.6 cm	8	3¼″ × 3¼″ 8.1 cm × 8.1 cm

Center Star Block

Description	Cut	Size	Cut	Size
Star center	4	Template C	4	Template F
Background, corners	4	2½″ × 2½″ 6.2 cm × 6.2 cm	4	4½″ × 4½″ 11.2 cm × 11.2 cm
Star tip units:				
Background	1	3¼″ × 3¼″ 8.1 cm × 8.1 cm	1	5¼″ × 5¼″ 13.1 cm × 13.1 cm
Tips	2	3¼″ × 3¼″ 8.1 cm × 8.1 cm	2	5¼″ × 5¼″ 13.1 cm × 13.1 cm
Tips, highlight	1	3¼″ × 3¼″ 8.1 cm × 8.1 cm	1	5¼″ × 5¼″ 13.1 cm × 13.1 cm
To frame stars:				
Background, Center Star	2	5⅛″ × 5⅛″ 12.6 cm × 12.6 cm	2	9⅜″ × 9⅜″ 23.1 cm × 23.1 cm

(table continued)

Description	Miniature		Wallhanging	
	Cut	Size	Cut	Size
Borders				
Inner	4	Template A	4	Template D
	4	Template A–reverse	4	Template D–reverse
Outer	8	Template B	8	Template E

Making Quarter-Square Triangle Units

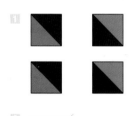

1. The Star tip units are made from quarter-square triangle units. They are simple to piece when you use half-square triangle units as the Parents. Use Method 1 on page 115 to make the half-square triangle units, but refer to the Cutting Chart for Star tip square sizes. Squares must be cut oversized to compensate for the diagonal seam that is sewn later to complete tip assembly. Pair a tip highlight square and a Star tip square to make Parent 1 units. Pair a background square and a Star tip square to make Parent 2 units. fig. 1

2. Parent 1 and Parent 2 units should measure exactly 1⅞" × 1⅞" (4.6 cm × 4.6 cm) for 3" (7.5 cm) Stars, 2⅞" × 2⅞" (7.1 cm × 7.1 cm) for 6" (15 cm) Stars, and 4⅞" × 4⅞" (12.1 cm × 12.1 cm) for 12" (30 cm) Stars. Draw a diagonal line from corner to corner on the reverse side of each Parent 1 unit. fig. 2

3. Pair a Parent 1 unit with a Parent 2 unit. Place right sides together, positioning squares so that darker Star tip fabric is facing a different fabric in the opposite square. Be sure all edges align. Use your fingertips to feel along the center seam—you should be able to tell if the seams are butting snugly against each other.

4. Sew two seams, each ¼" (0.6 cm) from the drawn center line, just as you did to construct the Parent units. Cut units apart on the drawn

line. Press each open to create Star tip units. Completed units for the 3″ (7.5 cm) Stars should measure 1½″ × 1½″ (3.7 cm × 3.7 cm); completed units for the 6″ (15 cm) Stars should measure 2½″ × 2½″ (6.2 cm × 6.2 cm); and completed units for the 12″ (30 cm) Star should measure 4½″ × 4½″ (11.2 cm × 11.2 cm).

To Make the Small Star Blocks

5. Position one center square, four background corner squares, and four Star tip units in three rows. Sew the components of each row together. Press seam allowances away from the Star tip units. Matching seams carefully, sew the rows together. Press seam allowances away from block center. Repeat to assemble a total of eight Small Star blocks. fig.

To Make the Center Square Block

6. With one exception, the Center Star is assembled in exactly the same way as the Small Stars. It has a pieced center. Using Template C for the miniature and Template F for the wallhanging, cut four identical triangles from your border print fabric.

7. Matching prints along their short sides, sew two triangles together. Press seam allowance to one side. Identical portions of the print should merge together at the seam. Repeat with two remaining triangles, pressing seam allowance in the opposite direction.

8. Sew the triangle pairs together diagonally to create a kaleidoscope center that measures 2½″ × 2½″ (6.2 cm × 6.2 cm) for the miniature or 4½″ × 4½″ (11.2 cm × 11.2 cm) for the wallhanging.

9. Sew the Center Star together, as in Step 5.

10. Cut each large background square in half once diagonally. Center and sew one of the resulting triangles to each side of the large Star. Press seams away from the Star. fig.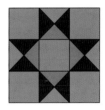

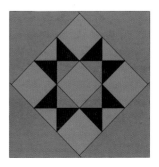

Making the Borders

11. To make the inner border, select a border print stripe that finishes at 2⅛″ (5.4 cm) wide for the miniature or 4¾″ (10.8 cm) wide for the wallhanging. Add seam allowances, cutting 2⅝″ (6.7 cm) strips for the miniature or 4¾″ (12.1 cm) strips for the wallhanging. Make a plastic copy of Template A for the miniature or Template E for the wallhanging. Border strips meet only at the inner corners of the quilt, so determine template placement based on the image you wish to create at those corners. Position the template on the fabric, aligning its long edges with the edges of the strip. Trim the fabric to match the angled edges of the template. Repeat, cutting three more identical images, using the first piece as a guide to template placement.

12. Cut four reversed patches. These are mirror images of those from Step 11. Turn an original patch over on top of the border strip, aligning the prints to achieve a perfect match. Place the reversed template on top to keep fabrics from shifting. Mark and cut.

    ✄ Sewing Tip

13. To make the outer border, first make a paper or plastic copy of Template B for the miniature or Template D for the wallhanging. Place the template on top of the outer border strips. Cut angles in fabric to match ends of template. Cut a total of eight.

Assembling the Quilt Top

14. Read page 122 about set-in seams. Sew an inner border strip piece and inner reversed border print piece to opposite sides of a Small Star block, ending seams at seam intersections to allow a piece to be set in later. Backstitch. Repeat to make four units.

    fig. 5

    ✄ Accuracy Check

15. Sew an outer border piece to the left side of a unit, leaving the beginning seam intersection unsewn as indicated by the dots. Stop sewing when you reach the intersection left open in Step 14. Remove the unit from the machine and align the short edge with the side of the block. Beginning where you stopped sewing the first seam, sew the two together, continuing to the ends of both pieces. fig. 6

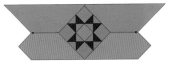

16. Attach an outer border piece to the opposite side, leaving seam open as indicated by the dot to the right of the last diagram. Repeat with remaining border units to make a total of four units.

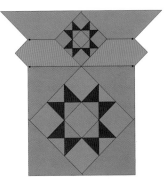

17. Sew one of these units to one side of the Center Star unit, beginning and ending each seam at outermost seam intersections. Repeat, sewing the remaining units to the center medallion. fig. 7

18. Match prints where borders meet at corners. Sew up the corner miters, beginning the seam at the exact spot where you stopped sewing in Step 17 and continuing to the ends of the strips.

19. Use the same technique to set-in a Small Star block at each corner of the quilt. Refer to page 122 if you need more help with setting-in.

Finishing the Quilt

20. Mark the top for quilting.

21. To sandwich, quilt, and bind, see page 155.

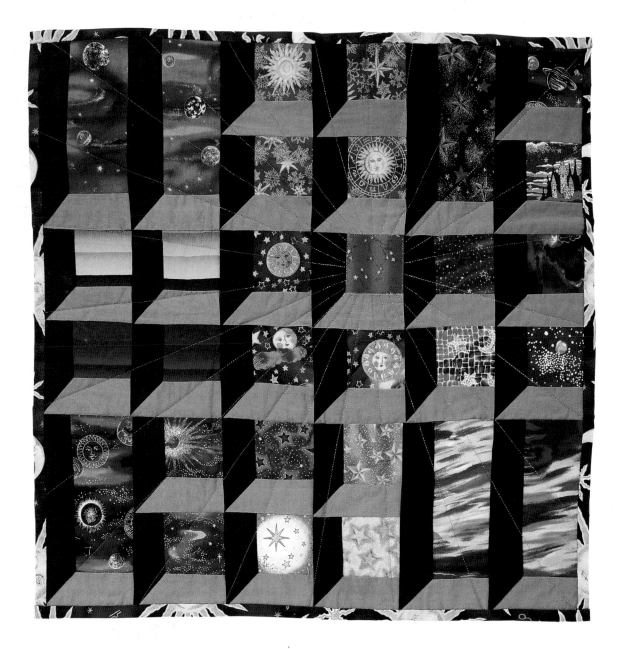

Mother's Fantasy Windows

	Miniature	Small lap
Finished quilt	12½" × 12½"	24½" × 24½"
	31.2 cm × 31.2 cm	61.2 cm × 61.2 cm
Window blocks	4" × 4"	8" × 8"
	10 cm × 10 cm	20 cm × 20 cm

This is a variation of the traditional Attic Windows block. Instead of single windows side by side, our blocks are each composed of varying Window sizes in the three layouts shown. Select one or more pictorial fabrics to fill your Windows. Sills are sewn from two fabrics, one darker, to give the appearance of depth when mitered corners are joined.

Back to Basics

Setting-In, see page 122

Color Value, see page 98

Fabric Requirements *(selvage to selvage)*

	Miniature	Small lap
Windowsill Blocks		
Windows, pictorial fabric	⅛ yard	¼ yard
	0.1 meter	0.2 meter
Dark windowsills	⅛ yard	¼ yard
	0.1 meter	0.2 meter
Medium windowsills	⅛ yard	¼ yard
	0.1 meter	0.2 meter
Finishing		
Backing	½ yard	⅞ yard
	0.4 meter	0.7 meter
Batting	16" × 16"	28" × 28"
	40 cm × 40 cm	71 cm × 71 cm
Binding (running)	65"	110"
	165 cm	279 cm

Variation One

Variation Two

Variation Three

Cutting Chart

Description	Miniature		Small lap	
	Cut	Size for miniature	Cut	Size for small lap
30 Window Blocks				
Square windows	24	1¾" × 1¾" 4.3 cm × 4.3 cm	24	3" × 3" 7.5 cm × 7.5 cm
Rectangular windows	6	1¾" × 3¾" 4.3 cm × 9.3 cm	6	3" × 7" 7.5 cm × 17.5 cm
Sills				
Dark strips	3	1¼" wide 3.1 cm wide	5	2" wide 5 cm wide
Medium strips	2	1¼" wide 3.1 cm wide	4	2" wide 5 cm wide

Making the Windows

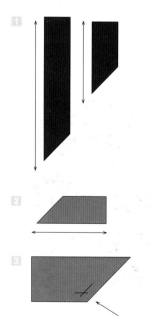

1. Use the strips of dark fabric to cut side sills for all blocks. Square up one end of a strip. Use your rotary ruler to make a 45° cut. Measure lengths carefully. The long sills are exactly 4⅞" (12.1 cm) for the miniature or 8⅞" (22.2 cm) for the lap quilt on their longest edge; the short sills are exactly 2⅞" (7.1 cm) for the miniature or 4⅞" (12.1 cm) for the lap quilt. Cut 6 long sills and 24 short sills. fig. 1

2. Use the strips of medium fabric to cut bottom sills for all blocks. The bottom sills are exactly 2⅞" (7.1 cm) for the miniature or 4⅞" (12.1 cm) for the lap on their longest edge. Notice that angled ends of side and bottom sills are mirror images. Cut 30 bottom sills. fig. 2

3. Mark inner seam intersections on the reverse side of each sill. Make a paper template to match the angled end, and measure ¼" (0.6 cm) inward from each edge to determine seam intersection. Punch a hole in the template at that spot with an icepick. Align the template

with the ending edge of each sill, and mark through the hole. Turn the template over to mark the opposite end of the sill. fig. 3

Making the Window Blocks

4. Sew a side and bottom sill together along their angled edges, beginning at the outer tips and ending at the marked seam intersection. Backstitch and remove from machine. Press seam open. fig. 4

5. Measure ¼″ (0.6 cm) inward on two edges to mark the seam intersection on one corner of a patch. Match it to the bottom sill, aligning square edges flush and matching the marked seam intersection with where you stopped sewing at the mitered end. Sew toward the miter, ending the seam there. Leave the needle down. fig. 5

6. Pivot and align the patch with the side sill, matching seam intersections. Sew to the end of the patches. Press seams toward sills. Repeat Steps 4 and 5 to assemble all Window units.

    ✂ Sewing Tip

7. Sew together individual units to form blocks. Assemble two Variation One blocks, five Variation Two blocks, and two Variation Three blocks.

Sewing Tip

If you have a difficult time pivoting small patches, set-in using two separate seams as described on page 122.

Assembling the Quilt Top

8. Arrange and sew the blocks into three rows, each row containing three blocks. Match seams carefully. fig. 6

9. Press seam allowances in adjoining rows in opposite directions, and then sew the rows together, matching seam intersections. Press.

Finishing the Quilt

10. Mark the top for quilting.

11. To sandwich, quilt, and bind, see page 155.

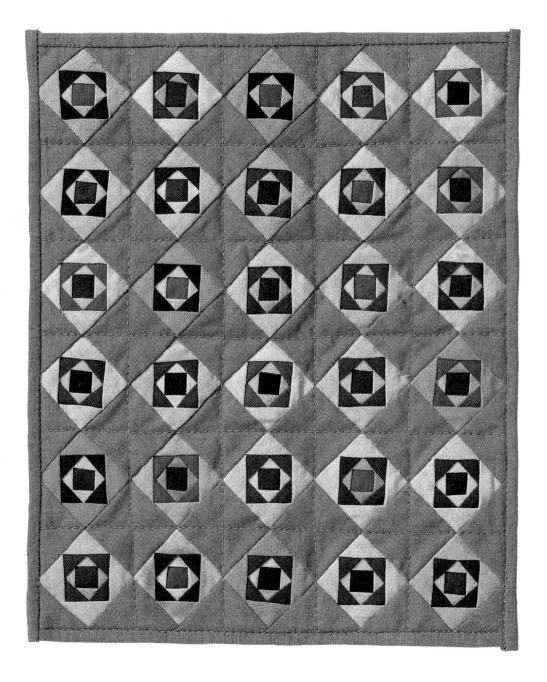

Little Amish Squares

Description	Size
Finished quilt	7½″ × 9″
	(18.7 cm × 22.2 cm)
Square-in-a-Square blocks	1″ × 1″
	(2.5 cm × 2.5 cm)

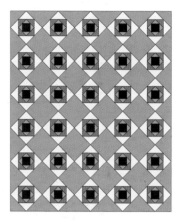

This quilt and the next, *Half Log Cabin*, are dollhouse quilts—made to a scale of 1 in 12. Each block finishes at 1″ × 1″ (2.5 cm × 2.5 cm), or nearly 1½″ × 1½″ (3.8 cm × 3.8 cm) wide if placed on-point, as photographed. Do you want additional blocks to drape over the mattress at the sides and the foot of the bed? If so, determine how far you wish them to drape on each side and add the extra blocks to your layout. Our quilt fits most double-sized beds. It is sewn with light to dark solids in the scrappy, Amish style, but the choice of fabric is up to you. This Square-in-a-Square block can be very effective if you take advantage of the differences in color value among chosen fabrics.

Back to Basics

An Introduction to Dollhouse Miniatures, see page 169
Foundation-Piecing Basic, see page 131
Color Value, see page 98

Fabric Requirements *(selvage to selvage)*

Description	Cut
Square-in-a-Square Blocks	
Scraps	⅓ yard
	0.3 meter
Finishing	
Backing	10″ × 12″
	25 cm × 30 cm
Batting (silk or thin cotton)	10″ × 12″
	25 cm × 30 cm
Binding	See page 170

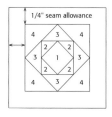

1/4" seam allowance

Cutting Chart

Description	Cut	Size
30 Square-in-a-Square Blocks		
Centers	30	7/8" × 7/8"
		2.2 cm × 2.2 cm
To make triangles:*		
Row 2	60	1 1/2" × 1 1/2"
		3.8 cm × 3.8 cm
Row 3	60	1 5/8" × 1 5/8"
		4.1 cm × 4.1 cm
Row 4	60	1 3/4" × 1 3/4"
		4.4 cm × 4.4 cm
Setting		
Setting squares, dark	20	1 1/2" × 1 1/2"
		3.8 cm × 3.8 cm
Setting triangles	5	3" × 3"
		7.5 cm × 7.5 cm
Corner triangles	2	2" × 2"
		5 cm × 5 cm

*Try cutting all squares the same size: 1 3/4" × 1 3/4" (4.4 cm × 4.4 cm). This creates waste but saves time.

Accuracy Check

As you add triangles, it is important to make sure edges extend past all printed lines that will later become seam lines. If patches tend to twist off-center, sew triangles to opposite sides of the row first, and then sew the remaining pair of opposite triangles.

1. Use Foundation Template A on page 171 to make 30 paper foundations.

2. Select a square of fabric for Piece 1. The size need not be exact. It should cover the square, plus provide enough overlap for a stable seam allowance on all sides.

3. Position the square right side up on the reverse (unprinted) side of the foundation, centering it on top of the area for Piece 1. Secure with a pin or a dab of glue stick. Hold the foundation up to the light, printed side facing you. You should be able to see a shadow of the

fabric square. Does it overlap all lines for Piece 1? Is the overlap enough to create a ⅛" (0.3 cm) seam allowance when those lines are sewn? fig. 1

4. Select a fabric for the triangles in Row 2. Cut two squares in half once diagonally. fig. 2

5. Center a triangle right side down on top of Piece 1, aligning edges. fig. 3

6. Holding fabrics in place, turn the foundation over. Sew directly on the line that separates Piece 1 from the long edge of the triangle being sewn in Row 2, beginning and ending two or three stitches on either side of the line. Remove the foundation from the machine and turn it over. To avoid pulling out threads, hold the seam in place with your fingers as you remove the block. fig. 4

7. Trim the seam allowance if necessary to reduce bulk, leaving approximately ⅛" (0.3 cm). Flip the triangle right side up. Finger-press in place. Be sure the outer, short edges of the triangle extend past the printed lines that define its shape by at least ⅛" (0.3 cm). fig. 5

8. Add the next triangle in Row 2 (moving in any direction you wish). Position the triangle right side down as with the first, aligning its edges with the connecting edge of Piece 1. fig. 6

9. Holding fabrics in place, flip the foundation over and sew on the line that separates the new triangle from Piece 1, beginning and ending two or three stitches on either side. Notice that sewing lines intersect, which helps stabilize each seam. fig. 7

10. Trim back the new seam allowance and the excess corner of the first triangle that lies under it. Flip the new triangle right side up. Finger-press triangle in place. fig. 8

✂ *Accuracy Check, page 58*

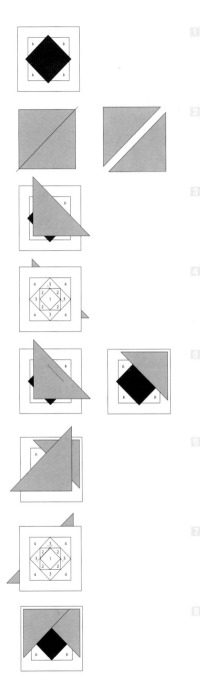

Speeding Things Along

Chain piecing makes this quilt go together faster. Have all triangles and foundations ready. Sew a triangle to the first block. Pull the threads slightly to move it out of the way, and continue sewing the next block. Keep going until you have sewn the first two pieces to each block. Remove the chained units from the machine and clip threads that tie them together. Trim all seam allowances, and begin chain piecing again, adding the second triangle to all blocks. Continue until all pieces are sewn to all blocks.

11. Add the remaining triangles in Row 2 in the same manner. fig. 9

12. Select a fabric for the triangles in Row 3. Cut two squares in half once diagonally as in Step 4.

13. Align a Row 3 triangle right side down on the reverse side of your foundation. Turn to the front side of the foundation and sew on the line separating it from Row 2. fig. 10

14. Trim seam allowance, cutting through any excess fabric in underlying triangles. Flip the new triangle right side up. Finger-press in place. fig. 11

15. Work in a circular motion to add the remaining triangles in Row 3 in the same manner. fig. 12

16. Select a fabric for the triangles in Row 4. Cut two squares in half once diagonally as in Step 4.

17. Sew Row 4 triangles to the foundation in the same manner as Row 3 triangles.

18. Use a medium-hot iron to press the block lightly. Do not remove papers.

19. Cut through the template and fabrics on the outer edge of the outermost printed line. fig. 13

20. Assemble all 30 blocks. Do not remove papers.

✂ Speeding Things Along

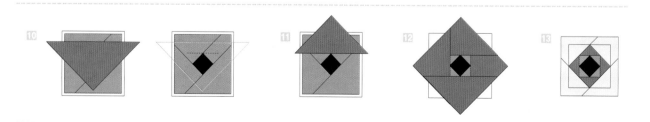

Assembling the Quilt Top

21. For corner triangles, cut each 2″ (4.8 cm) square in half once diagonally as in Step 4. For setting triangles, cut each 3″ (7.5 cm) square in half twice diagonally

22. Arrange pieced blocks, setting squares, and setting triangles in diagonal rows. Sew each row together.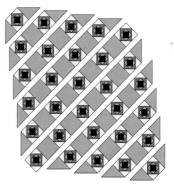

23. Remove papers from sewn seam allowances only. Press seam allowances toward the setting squares and triangles. If too bulky, press seams open.

24. Match seam intersections carefully and sew the diagonal rows together, using the foundation's printed seam line as a guide to a ¼″ (0.6 cm) seam allowance. Remove paper from the sewn seam allowances. Press.

25. Center and sew a corner triangle to each corner of the quilt.

26. The corner and setting triangles were cut oversized. Trim back if desired, leaving a ¼″ (0.6 cm) seam allowance around outer edge of quilt. Alternatively, trim only slightly to square up. Leaving extra width around the edges makes the blocks appear to float.

27. If you do not plan to use borders, remove all papers now. Tweezers may make the job easier; another trick is to start tears by running over the paper with a seamstress' tracing wheel.

28. Refer to "An Introduction to Dollhouse Miniatures," beginning on page 169, to finish your quilt.

Half Log Cabin

Description	Size
Finished quilt, with cutouts at footboard	5″ × 7″ (12.5 cm × 17.5 cm)
Half Log Cabin blocks	1″ × 1″ (2.5 cm × 2.5 cm)

Popular as early as the 1860s, the Log Cabin block is an all-time favorite. Though there are several methods of construction, we used foundation-piecing techniques, a wonderful time-saver. Our quilt is a traditional straight-furrows pattern and made in a dollhouse size, to a scale of 1 in 12. Log Cabin blocks are traditionally sewn with a combination of light and dark fabrics. Since the patches are tiny, you can use very small scraps. Sort your fabric by value. If making blocks with the traditional light half and dark half, like ours, keep in mind that all lights do not have to match exactly in value, nor do all darks. What's important is that opposite sides contrast and fabrics in same sides blend.

Fabric Requirements *(selvage to selvage)*

Description	Size
Half Log Cabin Blocks	
Scraps	⅜ yard 0.3 meter
Finishing	
Backing	10″ × 10″ 25 cm × 25 cm
Batting (silk or thin cotton)	10″ × 10″ 25 cm × 25 cm
Binding	See page 170

Back to Basics

An Introduction to Dollhouse Miniatures, see page 169
Foundation-Piecing Basics, see page 131
Color Value, see page 98

Cutting Chart

Description	Cut	Size
Scrappy strips, light*	24	¾" × 10" 2 cm × 25 cm
Scrappy strips, dark*	26	¾" × 10" 2 cm × 25 cm
Paper foundations	47	Template A

*Use longer strips to equal same total length if a less scrappy quilt is desired.

Making the Half Log Cabin Blocks

1. Use Foundation Template A on page 171 to make 35 paper foundations.

2. Set your sewing machine to sew a slightly shorter than normal stitch. Stitches should be short enough to remain stable when foundations are removed from the quilt after assembly but not so small that they cause bunching or unnecessary wear on the fabric. Nor should they be so small that they are impossible to remove if an error is made.

3. Select a dark fabric for Log 1. Cut an approximate ¾" × ¾" (2 cm × 2 cm) square. The size need not be exact. Your goal is for the fabric to cover the log, plus provide enough overlap for a stable seam allowance along all sides.

4. Position the square right side up on the reverse (unprinted) side of the foundation, centering it on top of the area for Log 1. Use a pin or a bit of glue stick to hold the fabric in place. Hold the foundation up to the light, printed side facing you. You should be able to see a shadow of the fabric square. Does it overlap all lines for Log 1? Is the overlap enough to create a stable seam allowance when those lines are sewn? The square must also extend slightly past the template's bottom printed edge. fig. 1

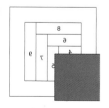

5. Select a light fabric for Log 2 and cut a ¾″ × ¾″ (2 cm × 2 cm) square. Position it right side down on top of Log 1, aligning edges. The new fabric completely covers Log 1. fig. 2

   ......✂ *Patch Dimensions*

6. Holding fabrics in place, turn the foundation over. Sew directly on the line that separates Log 1 from Log 2, beginning and ending two or three stitches on either side of the line. Remove the foundation from the machine. fig. 3

7. Trim the seam allowance if necessary to reduce bulk, leaving approximately ⅛″ (0.3 cm). Flip Log 2 right side up. Finger-press in place. Be sure the edges of Log 2 extend past all printed lines that border its shape, including the outermost line of the template. fig. 4

8. Select a dark fabric for Log 3, which runs vertically alongside Logs 1 and 2. Align the strip right side down on top of Logs 1 and 2. The left edge of the patch should extend approximately ¼″ (0.6 cm) past the vertical line separating Logs 1 and 2 from Log 3 (the seam line). Holding fabrics in place, flip the foundation over and sew on the line, beginning and ending two or three stitches on either side. fig. 5

9. Trim back the new seam allowance to approximately ⅛″ (0.3 cm), and then flip Log 3 right side up. Finger-press log in place. fig. 6

Patch Dimensions

One advantage of foundation piecing is that patches do not need to be cut to exact sizes. Some people like to work with long strips of fabric, sewing the end of the strip to the block and then trimming away the excess length. Others prefer to begin with smaller pieces that are closer to the actual size required for each patch. Determine patch size by keeping log dimensions and seam allowances in mind. The finished width of logs in this block is not quite ¼″ (0.6 cm). Allowing for a standard ¼″ (0.6 cm) seam allowance on each side means that no patch need be more than ¾″ (2 cm) wide. The longest finished length is 1″ (2.5 cm), so 1¾″–2″ long (4.4 cm) patches will allow you to piece any log in the block and still overlap the foundation's outer seam allowance.

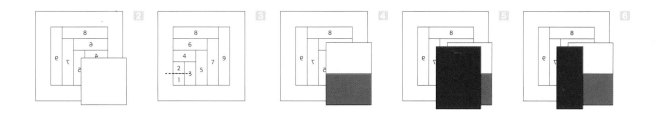

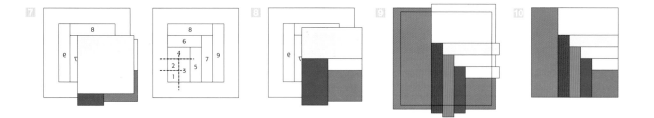

10. Log 4 is added in the same manner as previous logs. Align a light strip right side down, its upper edge extending approximately ¼" (0.6 cm) past the horizontal line separating the tops of Logs 2 and 3 from Log 4. Flip to the front side of the foundation and sew on the line, beginning and ending a few stitches on either side. fig. 7

11. Trim seam allowance, and flip Log 4 right side up. Finger-press log in place. fig. 8

12. Continue adding remaining logs in exactly the same manner, working in numerical order. When you reach the final logs, be sure your patches are wide enough so that when flipped right side up each log stretches past the outer printed line of the template. The outer-most line is visible here, to illustrate the overlap. fig. 9

13. Press the block.

14. Cut through all layers at the outermost edge of the outer printed line. fig. 10

15. Assemble 35 blocks. Do not remove papers.

Assembling the Quilt Top

16. Arrange blocks in rows. Match edges carefully and sew blocks in each row together. Remove papers from the sewn seam allowances only. Press seams in adjoining rows in opposite directions, or press open to reduce bulk. fig.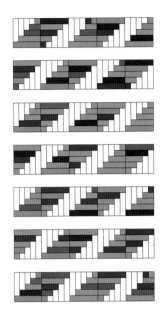

17. Pin and sew rows together, matching seam intersections carefully as you work. Be sure to sew on the long printed line created when blocks were joined into rows. Remove papers from seam allowances. Press open or to one side.

18. If you do not plan to use borders, remove all papers now.

19. Refer to "An Introduction to Dollhouse Miniatures," beginning on page 169, to finish your quilt.

Pitchers for Tildy's Cabin

	Miniature	Small Lap
Finished quilt	15¾" × 15¾"	29½" × 29½"
	40 cm × 40 cm	75 cm × 75 cm
Pitcher blocks	3¾" × 3¾"	7" × 7"
	8.5 cm × 8.5 cm	17.8 cm × 17.8 cm
Courthouse Steps blocks	3¾" × 3¾"	7" × 7"
	8.5 cm × 8.5 cm	17.8 cm × 17.8 cm

Donna once made Janet a king-sized bed quilt using a larger version of our pitcher and bowls design, which was inspired by a piece in Janet's collection of spongeware pottery. For our smaller versions, we added foundation-pieced Courthouse Steps blocks, a variation of Log Cabin blocks. We placed them on point with our pitchers. Half Courthouse Steps replace setting triangles around the quilt's edge, and quarter blocks complete the corners.

Back to Basics

Appliqué Basics, see page 139
Foundation-Piecing Basics, see page 131
Color Value, see page 98

Fabric Requirements *(selvage to selvage)*

	Miniature	Small lap
Pitcher Blocks		
Background squares	⅛ yard	½ yard
	0.1 meter	0.4 meter
Pitchers, nine scraps	3" × 3"	4" × 4"
	7.5 cm × 7.5 cm	10 cm × 10 cm
Bowls, nine scraps	2" × 4"	3" × 6"
	5 cm × 10 cm	7.5 cm × 15 cm

(table continued)

	Miniature	Small lap

Courthouse Steps Blocks*

Light logs	½ yard	1 yard
	0.4 meter	*0.9 meter*
Medium logs	½ yard	1 yard
	0.4 meter	*0.9 meter*
Center squares, dark	⅛ yard	⅛ yard
	0.1 meter	*0.1 meter*

Finishing

Backing	½ yard	1 yard
	0.4 meter	*0.9 meter*
Batting	17″ × 17″	34″ × 34″
	43 cm × 43 cm	*86 cm × 86 cm*
Binding (running)	65″	125″
	165 cm	*317 cm*

For foundation materials required, see page 132.

Cutting Chart

	Miniature		Small lap	
Description	*Cut*	*Size for miniature*	*Cut*	*Size for small lap*

Nine Pitcher Blocks

Background square	9	3¾″ × 3¾″	9	7″ × 7″
		9.3 cm × 9.3 cm		*17.5 cm × 17.5 cm*
Pitchers	9	Template A-1	9	Template B-1
Bowls	9	Template A-2	9	Template B-2

Nine Courthouse Steps Blocks *

Centers, complete blocks	4	1¼″ × 1¼″	4	2″ × 2″
		3.2 cm × 3.2 cm		*5 cm × 5 cm*
Large triangles, half blocks	2	2½″ × 2½″	2	3½″ × 3½″
		6.4 cm × 6.4 cm		*9.2 cm × 9.2 cm*

Description	Miniature			Small lap	
	Cut	Size for miniature		Cut	Size for small lap
Small triangles, quarter blocks	2	1¾″ × 1¾″ 4.4 cm × 4.4 cm		2	2¼″ × 2¼″ 5.7 cm × 5.7 cm
Light Logs, strips	14	1″ 2.5 cm		26	1¼″ 3.2 cm
Medium Logs, strips	14	1″ 2.5 cm		26	1¼″ 3.2 cm

*Four complete blocks, eight half blocks, and four quarter blocks.

Paper Foundations

Complete blocks	4	Template A-3		4	Template B-3
Half blocks	8	Template A-4		8	Template B-4
Quarter blocks	4	See instructions		4	See instructions

To Make the Pitcher Blocks

1. Read Appliqué Basics, beginning on page 139. Use Templates A-1 and A-2 to cut Pitcher pieces for the miniature or Templates B-1 and B-2 for the lap quilt. After selecting an appliqué method, center pieces on background squares as shown in the layout diagram on page 69. Appliqué them to the squares. Be sure to tuck the unfinished bottom edge of the Pitcher under the top lip of the bowl. Make nine blocks.

To Make the Complete Courthouse Steps Blocks

2. Set your machine to sew a slightly shorter than normal stitch. Stitches should be short enough to remain stable when foundations are removed after assembly, but not so small that they cause bunching, unnecessary wear on the fabric, or become impossible to

remove if an error is made. Make four foundations using Template A-3 for the miniature or Template B-3 for the lap quilt.

✂ Patch Dimensions

3. Position a dark center square right side up on the reverse (unprinted) side of a full block foundation, centering it on top of the area for Log 1. Use a pin or a bit of glue stick to hold the fabric in place. Hold the foundation up to the light, printed side facing you. You should be able to see a shadow of the fabric square. Does it overlap all lines for Log 1? Is the overlap enough to create a stable seam allowance when those lines are sewn? If not, reposition and check again. fig. 1

4. Select a medium fabric for Log 2. Use a long strip, or cut a segment ½" (1.2 cm) longer than Log 2. Position the strip right side down on top of the center square, aligning its left edge with the square. fig. 2

5. Holding fabrics in place, turn the foundation over. Sew directly on the line that separates the center square from Log 2, beginning and ending two or three stitches on either side of the line. fig. 3

6. Trim the seam allowance if necessary to reduce bulk. Flip Log 2 fabric side up. Be sure all unsewn edges of Log 2 extend past the printed lines that define that log. The overlap must be wide enough to create stable seam allowances when seams are sewn later. fig. 4

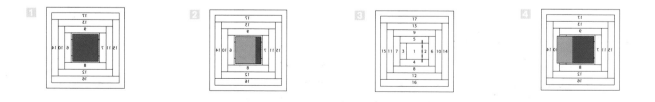

7. Select a medium fabric for Log 3. Align the strip right side down along the right side edge of the center log. Flip the foundation over and sew on the line that separates the two, beginning and ending two or three stitches on either side. fig.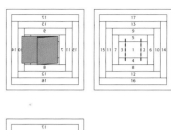

8. Trim back the new seam allowance if necessary to reduce bulk, then flip Log 3 fabric side up. Finger-press log in place. fig.

9. Log 4 is added in the same manner as previous logs. Align a light strip right side down, its lower edge aligned with the lower edges of Logs 1 to 3. Flip to the front side of the foundation and sew on the line separating the pieces, beginning and ending a few stitches on either side. fig.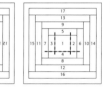

10. Trim seam allowance, and flip Log 4 fabric side up. Finger-press log in place. fig.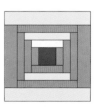

11. Continue adding remaining logs in exactly the same manner, working in numerical order. When you reach the outer logs, be sure the patches are positioned so that when flipped right side up each log stretches slightly past the outer printed line of the template.

12. Use a medium-hot iron to press the block lightly.

13. Cut through all layers along the outermost edge of the outer printed line. This step automatically creates an exact ¼″ (0.6 cm) seam allowance around the block's perimeter. fig.

14. Assemble four whole Courthouse Steps blocks. Do not remove papers.

To Make the Half Blocks

15. Make eight foundations using Template A-4 or Template B-4. When making foundations, consider which logs should be light and which should be medium. Our light side is made up of Strips 3, 5, 7, and 9.

If you duplicate the template and sew light strips to those positions, you will have the correct layout for only four of the eight blocks required. That is because you are working with mirror images of a block that is not symmetrical. To solve the problem, draw four foundation templates to match the image of the original template and draw four more that are its reverse. We recommend sheer tracing paper. Sew on the front side of four foundations and sew on the back side of the rest. You should be able to see marked lines clearly through the thin paper. Use a permanent marker that won't rub off onto fabrics placed against marked lines.

16. Cut each of the squares reserved for dark center logs in half twice diagonally. fig. 10

17. Center the triangle for Log 1 on the reverse side of the template, making sure its short edges overlap marked seam lines and that its long edge overlaps the outer printed line of the foundation.

18. Use fabric strips to add logs in numerical order in the same manner as for the whole blocks. Allow extra length at the ends of each log to compensate for the diagonal block edges.

19. Press the finished block and trim on the outermost line. Make three more identical half blocks.

20. Make four blocks of the reverse image, positioning fabric on the marked side and sewing on the unmarked side of tracing paper.

......✂ Sewing Tip

To Make the Quarter Blocks

21. Position tracing paper against a half block template, A-4 or B-4. Draw a diagonal line from corner to midpoint of long edge. fig. 11

22. Trace all lines to the left of the diagonal line. Draw a second diagonal line parallel to the first, and exactly ¼″ (0.6 cm) from it.

Sewing Tip

When we cut setting triangles from plain fabric, we use the same method as Step 16, so that the straight grain ends up on each triangle's longest edge. Because we used straight grain strips in our half blocks and their ends are cut at an angle, those ends are bias cuts. Using bias strips for the Logs in our half blocks would give us straight grain along the edges, but they are stretchy to work with. To help stabilize the bias edges, fold back the foundation paper along the seam allowance and stitch a seam about ⅛″ (0.3 cm) inward along the entire diagonal edge of the block.

Extend original outer template lines to meet the second diagonal. Make a total of four corner foundations. fig. 12

23. Cut each of the squares reserved for dark centers in half once on the diagonal. fig. 13

24. Piece and trim four corner blocks in the same manner as others.

Assembling the Quilt Top

25. Arrange blocks into diagonal rows. Sew blocks in each row together. Remove papers from the sewn seam allowances of foundation blocks. Press seam allowances toward the appliqué blocks. fig. 14

26. Pin and sew rows together, matching seam intersections carefully. Sew the four corners to the quilt. Remove all remaining papers and press the quilt. To avoid stretching blocks, take care when removing papers, especially around the outer edges.

Finishing the Quilt

27. Mark the top for quilting.

28. To sandwich, quilt, and bind, see page 155.

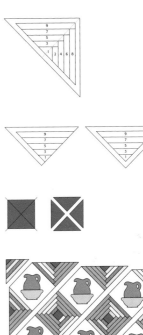

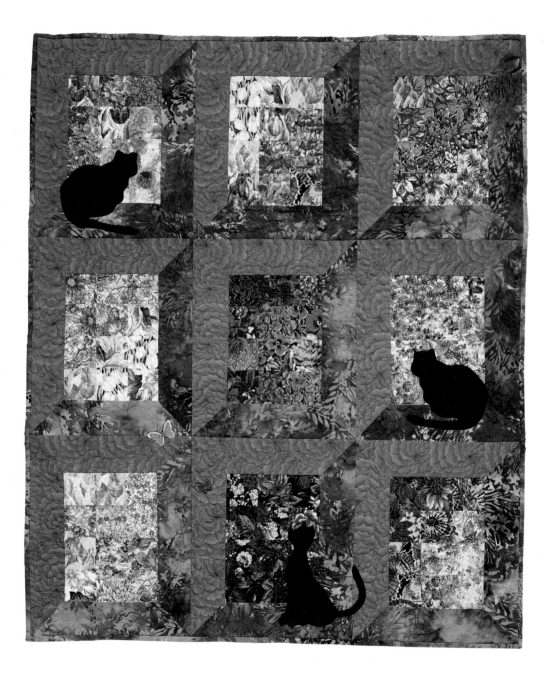

Catching the View

	Miniature	Lap
Finished quilt	17″ × 20″	33½″ × 39½″
	42.9 cm × 50.4 cm	84.6 cm × 99.6 cm
Windowsill blocks	5½″ × 6½″	11″ × 13″
	13.9 cm × 16.4 cm	27.8 cm × 32.8 cm

The central rectangles in the blocks of this lap quilt are each pieced with a set of 12 floral squares in the watercolor style, then surrounded by dark and medium mitered strips. Appliquéd cats perch in some of the windows, and one has his eyes on a flock of butterflies. Because they are much smaller, each window in the miniature variation is cut from a single fabric, rather than pieced.

Fabric Requirements *(selvage to selvage)*

	Miniature	Lap
Windowsill Blocks		
Floral squares, scraps	¼ yard	⅝ yard
	0.2 meter	0.5 meter
Medium windowsills	¼ yard	⅝ yard
	0.2 meter	0.5 meter
Dark windowsills	¼ yard	⅝ yard
	0.2 meter	0.5 meter
Appliqué Silhouettes		
Cats, three dark prints	4″ × 4″	8″ × 8″
	10 cm × 10 cm	20 cm × 20 cm
Butterfly, three prints	1½″ × 1½″	2½″ × 2½″
	3.7 cm × 3.7 cm	6.2 cm × 6.2 cm

(table continued)

Back to Basics

Appliqué Basics, see page 139

Setting-In, see page 122

Color Value, see page 98

		Miniature		Lap

Finishing

	Miniature	Lap
Backing	⅝ yard *0.5 meter*	1 yard *0.9 meter*
Batting	21″ × 24″ *53 cm × 61 cm*	36″ × 42″ *91 cm × 107 cm*
Binding (running)	85″ *216 cm*	160″ *406 cm*

Cutting Chart

		Miniature		Lap
Description	*Cut*	*Size for miniature*	*Cut*	*Size for lap*

Nine Windowsill Blocks

Floral squares	9	1½″ × 1½″ *3.7 cm × 3.7 cm*	108	2½″ × 2½″ *6.2 cm × 6.2 cm*
Dark strips (width)	3	1¾″ *4.4 cm*	6	3″ *7.6 cm*
Medium strips (width)	3	1¾″ *4.4 cm*	6	3″ *7.6 cm*

Appliqué Silhouettes

Crouching cat	1	Template A	Template D
Crouching cat, reversed	1	Template A reverse	Template D reverse
Standing cat	1	Template B	Template E
Butterfly	1	Template C	Template F

Making the Windowsills

1. Use the strips of medium fabric to cut Windowsills for the top and left sides of the blocks. Use your rotary ruler to make two 45° cuts for each strip. Measure lengths between cuts carefully. The side sills are exactly 7¾″ (19.3 cm) for the miniature or 14¼″ (35.8 cm) for the lap quilt on their longest edge; the top sills are exactly 6¾″ (16.8 cm) for the miniature or 12¼″ (30.7 cm) for the lap quilt. Cut nine side sills and nine top sills. fig. 1

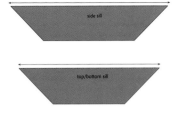

2. Cut nine side and nine bottom sills from the dark strips.

   Sewing Tip

3. Mark inner seam intersections on the reverse side of each strip. An easy way to do this is to make a paper template to match the end of each shape, and measure ¼″ (0.6 cm) inward on all sides of the short edges where set-in patches will occur. The intersection of lines indicates where you must stop sewing each seam. Use a hole punch or ice pick to punch out a hole at each spot. Align the template with the ending edge of each strip, and mark through the hole. Turn the template over to mark the opposite end of the strip. fig. 2

Sewing Tip

Cut and assemble the pieces for one block before cutting all strips required for your quilt.

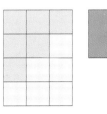

Making the Windowsill Blocks

4. Arrange Windowsill units in your design area as shown in the layout diagram. Note that medium Windowsill strips are used in the top and left positions, and dark strips on the right and bottom.

5. Place 12 floral squares within each rectangle formed by sills. You might have to overlap some squares to allow for unsewn seam allowances. For the miniature quilt, place one 3½″ × 4½″ (8.7 cm × 11.2 cm) rectangle within each window. fig. 3

6. Stand back and view the quilt. Are you satisfied with the layout? Try shifting squares to create shadows or highlights in different areas.

For instance, you can cluster colors, such as greens, to mimic trees and shrubs.

7. For the lap quilt, sew each set of squares together in four rows, each row containing three floral squares. Press seams in adjoining rows in opposite directions, and then sew the rows together, matching seams carefully. Press the rectangular units. For the miniature, the rectangles are cut to the correct size. Use a removable marker to mark seam intersections on the front of each rectangle. If setting-in is new to you, refer to page 122 before continuing.

.... ✄ Sewing Tip

8. Sew a medium top and a dark side sill together along their diagonal edges, beginning the seam at the outer point. Stop sewing at the inner, marked intersection and backstitch. Sew a medium side sill and a dark bottom sill together in the same way. Press seams open.

9. To set-in a floral rectangle, match the seam intersections on the lower-right edge of the rectangle with the marks on the right, unsewn edge of the dark bottom sill. Match the seam intersection on the lower-left edge of the rectangle with the point where the slit-like opening begins in the pressed-open seam between sills.

10. Begin sewing on the outer edge of the dark sill, with the sill on top as you sew. Stop sewing when you reach the seam intersection on the opposite edge of the sill, with the needle in the down position.

11. Pivot the fabrics. Match the seam intersections on the ends of both patches, and then match the edges along their entire lengths. Continue sewing, ending the seam at the matched points. Back-stitch and remove the unit from machine. Press seam allowances toward the sills.

12. Sew the unit containing the medium top and dark side sill to the rectangle in the same way, beginning the seam at the top left side of the upper sill. Press new seams toward the sills.

Sewing Tip

The rectangular units for your lap quilt should measure 6 1/2" × 8 1/2" (16.2 cm × 21.2 cm). If they are smaller than they should be, try pressing all seams open, rather than to one side. Match and sew seams carefully. If the rectangles are not accurate, your finished blocks will not be accurate either.

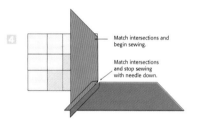

Match intersections and begin sewing.

Match intersections and stop sewing with needle down.

13. Sew up the miters to connect dark sills and medium sills, beginning at the point where seams meet on inner edges.

14. Repeat Steps 8 to 13 to assemble a total of nine blocks.

Assembling the Quilt Top

15. Arrange the blocks into three rows as shown in the layout diagram on page 77, each row containing three vertically set blocks.

16. Sew the blocks in each row together. Press seam allowances in adjoining rows in opposite directions, and then sew rows together, matching seam intersections carefully. Press the quilt.

Adding the Appliqué Silhouettes

17. Decide how many cats you would like. Read "Appliqué Basics," page 139. Make templates as directed, depending on the technique you select. Prepare the cat figures for appliqué. We made each of our cats from one piece of fabric, to resemble silhouettes. Templates are on page 177.

18. Decide how many butterflies you would like. We cut butterflies from two different prints, then appliquéd them to the quilt top. Alternatively, use Template C to make butterflies for the miniature or Template F for the lap. The simple shape can be cut from one fabric, or you can prepare the body from a small scrap and then tuck wings under it on each side. Machine-stitch or embroider antennae.

19. Pin or baste prepared figures to the quilt, and then appliqué using the method of your choice.

Finishing the Quilt

20. Mark the top for quilting.

21. To sandwich, quilt, and bind, see page 155.

Kittens with the Blues

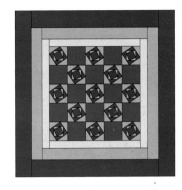

	Miniature	Lap
Finished quilt	22½" × 22½"	42½" × 42½"
	57.1 cm × 57.1 cm	108 cm × 108 cm
Skewed Square-in-a-Square blocks	2½" × 2½"	5" × 5"
	6.4 cm × 6.4 cm	12.7 cm × 12.7 cm

Try this little quilt for a quick and easy project. Donna surrounded her kitten squares with Skewed Square-in-a-Square blocks stitched in shades of blue. The kitten fabric is repeated in the outer border. The fabrics within skewed blocks can be identical from block to block or scrappy. Select fabrics that contrast with each other, and position them so that color value changes from row to row.

Back to Basics

Foundation-Piecing Basics, see page 131

Color Value, see page 98

Fabric Requirements *(selvage to selvage)*

	Miniature	Lap
Skewed Square-in-a-Square Blocks		
Assorted fabrics	¾ yard	1¼ yard
	0.6 meter	1.1 meter
Plain blocks, Plus Outer Border		
Pictorial fabric	½ yard	1⅛ yard
	0.4 meter	1 meter
Borders		
Inner border, light	⅛ yard	¼ yard
	0.1 meter	0.2 meter
Middle border, medium	⅛ yard	½ yard
	0.1 meter	0.4 meter

*For foundation materials required, see page 132.

(table continued)

	Miniature	Lap
Finishing		
Backing	⅞ yard *0.7 meter*	2¾ yards *2.5 meter*
Batting	28″ × 28″ *71 cm × 71 cm*	46″ × 46″ *117 cm × 117 cm*
Binding (running)	105″ *267 cm*	185″ *470 cm*

Cutting Chart

	Miniature		Lap	
Description	Cut	*Size for miniature*	Cut	*Size for small lap*
12 Plain Blocks				
Squares	12	3″ × 3″ *7.5 cm × 7.5 cm*	12	5½″ × 5½″ *14 cm × 14 cm*
Skewed Square-in-a-Square Blocks				
Centers	13	1½″ × 1½″ *3.7 cm × 3.7 cm*	13	2½″ × 2½″ *6.2 cm × 6.2 cm*
To make triangles:				
Row 2	26	1¼″ × 2¼″ *3.2 cm × 5.6 cm*	26	1¾″ × 3¼″ *4.4 cm × 8.1 cm*
Row 3	26	1¾″ × 2½″ *4.4 cm × 6.2 cm*	26	2½″ × 3¾″ *6.2 cm × 9.5 cm*
Row 4	26	2″ × 3″ *4.7 cm × 7.5 cm*	26	3¼″ × 4½″ *8.1 cm × 11.2 cm*
Borders				
Inner, straight set	2	1½″ wide *3.7 cm wide*	4	1½″ wide *3.7 cm wide*
Middle, straight set	2	2″ wide *5.1 cm wide*	4	3″ wide *7.5 cm wide*
Outer, straight set	4	2¾″ wide *6.9 cm wide*	4	5½″ wide *14 cm wide*

Making the Skewed Square-in-a-Square Blocks

1. Make 13 paper foundations using Foundation Template A for the miniature and B for the lap-sized quilt. See pages 171–172.

2. Cut rectangles reserved for the pieced blocks in half once diagonally. Remember that your block will be a mirror image of the front of the template. Unless you are using fabrics with no right or wrong side, triangles must be cut along opposite diagonals of the patches, depending on which row they will be sewn in. Row 2 and 4 triangles are cut in the same direction; Row 3 triangles are cut along the opposite diagonal. fig. 1

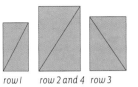

row 1   row 2 and 4   row 3

3. Position a center square right side up on the reverse (unprinted) side of a foundation, centering it. Its edges should be parallel to the printed edges of the piece, overlapping them by approximately ¼" (0.6 cm). Use a pin or a bit of glue stick to hold the fabric in place. Hold the foundation up to the light, printed side facing you. You should be able to see a shadow of the fabric square. If alignment is not correct, reposition and check again. fig. 2

4. Select a Row 2 triangle, and position it right side down on top of the center square. Positioning triangles like these on the foundation is a bit trickier than straight strips or right triangles. It may take a bit of practice for you to get it just right. fig. 3

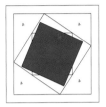

5. Holding fabrics in place, turn the foundation over. Sew directly on the line that separates the center piece from your new triangle, beginning and ending two or three stitches on either side of the line. fig. 4

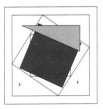

6. Flip the triangle fabric side up. All unsewn edges of the triangle must extend past the printed lines that define its shape. If placement is correct, trim back the seam allowance to reduce bulk, and press the triangle in place. fig. 5

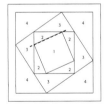

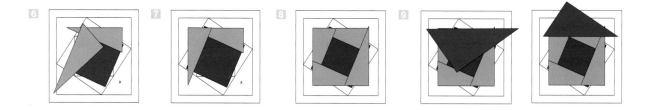

7. Select a second Row 2 triangle. Align it right side down along the next edge of the center square. Holding fabrics in place, flip the foundation over and sew on the line that separates the two, beginning and ending two or three stitches on either side. fig. 6

8. Check triangle position. Trim back the new seam allowance if necessary to reduce bulk, and then flip the patch right side up and finger-press in place. fig. 7

9. Add the two remaining triangles to Row 2 in the same manner. fig. 8

10. Select a Row 3 triangle, positioning it right side down. Turn to the front of the foundation and sew on the line separating it from the inner row, beginning and ending the seam a few stitches on either side of the line. Flip the triangle right side up and check placement. fig. 9

11. Add remaining Row 3 triangles. fig. 10

12. Add Row 4 triangles in the same manner, using the orientation as for Row 2. Press the block lightly.

13. Cut through all layers along the outermost edge of the outer printed line.

14. Assemble a total of thirteen skewed blocks. Do not remove papers.

Assembling the Quilt Top

15. Arrange blocks in five rows, each containing five blocks. Block types alternate in adjoining rows, as in the layout diagram. Sew the blocks in each row together. Remove papers from seam allowances of foundation-pieced blocks. Press seam allowances toward the plain squares.

16. Pin and sew rows together, matching seam intersections carefully. Remove papers from seam allowances and press.

17. Read "Working with Borders," beginning on page 149, to measure, cut, and add straight-set borders. Remove the remaining paper foundations.

Finishing the Quilt

18. Mark the top for quilting.

19. To sandwich, quilt, and bind, see page 155.

Walk Around the Block

	Small miniature	Miniature
Finished quilt	15½″ × 15½″	22″ × 22″
	39 cm × 39 cm	55.8 cm × 55.8 cm
Center Medallion	3¾″ × 3¾″	5″ × 5″
	9.5 cm × 9.5 cm	12.7 cm × 12.7 cm
Strip-pieced units	1⅛″ × 1⅛″	1½″ × 1½″
	2.8 cm × 2.8 cm	3.7 cm × 3.7 cm

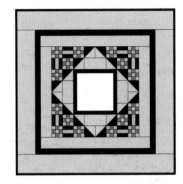

This little quilt is assembled entirely with quick-piecing techniques. Half-square triangle units frame the center Medallion, and strip-pieced Nine-Patch and bar blocks fill in the outer edges. The three-piece border repeats fabrics that surround the Medallion. Make it soft and muted as shown, or liven it up with bolder splashes of color. Pictorial fabrics are available in such a wide range of styles that you should have no problem finding a center Medallion to build the quilt around.

Back to Basics

Strip-Piecing Basics, see page 127
Rotary Cutting and Template Basics,
  see page 103
Machine-Piecing and Hand-Piecing
  Basics, see page 119

Fabric Requirements *(selvage to selvage)*

	Small miniature	Miniature
Center Medallion, pictorial	4¼″ × 4¼″	5½″ × 5½″
	10.7 cm × 10.7 cm	13.9 cm × 13.9 cm
Triangle units, frame and middle border, dark	¼ yard	¼ yard
	0.2 meter	0.2 meter
Triangle units, middle and outer borders, medium	¼ yard	¼ yard
	0.2 meter	0.2 meter
Strip-pieced blocks, light	⅛ yard	⅛ yard
	0.1 meter	0.1 meter
Nine-Patch blocks, medium	⅛ yard	⅛ yard
	0.1 meter	0.1 meter

(table continued)

	Small miniature	Miniature
Bar blocks, medium	⅛ yard	⅛ yard
	0.1 meter	*0.1 meter*

Finishing

	Small miniature	Miniature
Backing	½ yard	¾ yard
	0.4 meter	*0.6 meter*
Batting	16″ × 16″	26″ × 26″
	41 cm × 41 cm	*66 cm × 66 cm*
Binding (running)	62″	98″
	158 cm	*249 cm*

Cutting Chart

Description		Small miniature		Miniature
	Cut	Size	Cut	Size

Center Medallion Unit

Description	Cut	Size	Cut	Size
Center Medallion	1	4¼″ × 4¼″	1	5½″ × 5½″
		10.7 cm × 10.7 cm		*13.9 cm × 13.9 cm*
Vertical frame, center Medallion	2	⅞″ × 4¼″	2	1″ × 5½″
		2.2 cm × 10.7 cm		*2.5 cm × 13.9 cm*
Horizontal frame, center Medallion	2	⅞″ × 5″	2	1″ × 6½″
		2.2 cm × 12.7 cm		*2.5 cm × 16.4 cm*
Triangle unit links, medium	4	1⅝″ × 2¾″	4	2″ × 3½″
		4.1 cm × 7 cm		*5 cm × 8.9 cm*
Half-square triangle units:				
Medium	8	2″ × 2″	8	2⅜″ × 2⅜″
		5 cm × 5 cm		*5.9 cm × 5.9 cm*
Dark	8	2″ × 2″	8	2⅜″ × 2⅜″
		5 cm × 5 cm		*5.9 cm × 5.9 cm*

16 Nine-Patch Blocks

Description	Cut	Size	Cut	Size
Light	2	⅞″ × 29″	2	1″ × 33″
		2.2 cm × 74 cm		*2.5 cm × 83 cm*

Description	Small miniature		Miniature	
	Cut	Size	Cut	Size
Light	1	7/8″ × 15″	1	1″ × 17″
		2.2 cm × 38 cm		2.5 cm × 43 cm
Medium	1	7/8″ × 29″	1	1″ × 33″
		2.2 cm × 74 cm		2.5 cm × 83 cm
Medium	2	7/8″ × 15″	2	1″ × 17″
		2.2 cm × 38 cm		2.5 cm × 43 cm
Eight Bar Blocks				
Light	1	7/8″ × 10″	1	1″ × 17″
		2.2 cm × 23 cm		2.5 cm × 43 cm
Medium	2	7/8″ × 10″	2	1″ × 17″
		2.2 cm × 23 cm		2.5 cm × 43 cm
Borders				
Inner border, width	1	1½″	2	1½″
		3.7 cm		3.7 cm
Middle border, width, dark	2	1″	2	1¼″
		2.5 cm		3.1 cm
Outer border	2	2″	3	2½″
		5 cm		6.2 cm

Making the Medallion Unit

1. Align edges carefully and sew a short dark frame to the left and right sides of the center Medallion. Press seam allowances toward the Medallion. Sew a long dark frame to the top and bottom of the Medallion. Press seam allowances toward the Medallion.

2. Make 16 half-square triangle units from the medium and dark squares using Method 1 on page 115. When ready for block assembly, each half-square triangle unit should measure 1⅝″ × 1⅝″ (4.1 cm × 4.1 cm) for the small miniature or 2″ × 2″ (5 cm × 5 cm) for the miniature.

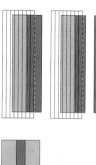

Making the Nine-Patch Blocks

3. Group the strips for the Nine-Patch blocks by length. Sew the three longest strips together lengthwise, with a medium strip in the middle. Press seam allowances toward the middle strip. fig. **1**

    ✂ *Sewing Tip*

4. Use your rotary-cutting equipment to square up one end of the strip set. Cut a total of 32 segments from the set. Segments for the small miniature are cut ⅞" (2.2 cm) long; segments for the miniature are cut 1" (2.5 cm) long. fig. **2**

5. Make a second strip set from the shorter strips, with the light strip in the center. Press seam allowances toward the dark strips. Square up one end of the strip set and cut 16 segments from it, using the lengths given in Step 4. fig. **3**

6. Sew two segments from Step 4 to each side of a Step 5 segment. Press seam allowances toward the center strip. Make a total of 16 Nine-Patch blocks. fig. **4**

Making the Bar Blocks

7. Sew the bar block strips together lengthwise, with darker strips on the outer edges. Press seam allowances toward the dark strips.

8. Square up one end of the strip set and cut eight segments from it. Cut segments for the small miniature 1⅝" (4.1 cm) long; cut segments for the miniature 2" (5 cm) long. fig. **5**

Sewing Tip

Unless they are trimmed, seam allowances in the small miniature will overlap, and seams in the miniature will meet. Before pressing seams to one side, press them flat, exactly as they were sewn. Use your rotary-cutting equipment to trim back each seam, leaving a ⅛" to 3/16" (0.3 cm to 0.4 cm) seam allowance. Trim back any time seam allowances create excess bulk.

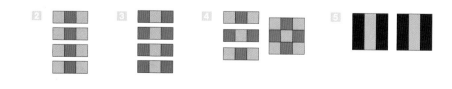

Assembling the Quilt Top

9. Arrange the pieces in groups. Sew pieces within each grouping into rows, and then sew rows together. Match all seams carefully, and press adjoining seam allowances in opposite directions. fig. 6

10. Sew the vertical columns to the left and right sides of the central Medallion, and then sew the top and bottom horizontal units to the quilt. Match seams carefully. Press.

11. To measure and add borders, see page 149. The Cutting Chart lists suggested strip widths for each quilt size. We used straight-sewn borders, repeating the fabric that surrounds the central Medallion in the inner and outer borders. Additional strip length is necessary for mitered borders (see page 151).

Finishing the Quilt

12. Mark the top for quilting.

13. To sandwich, quilt, and bind, see page 155.

CHAPTER 2

Fabric Basics

Though many fabrics can be used for quilting, we prefer to use 100 percent cotton fabrics and threads. Cotton wears well, is easy to work with, frays less than blended fabrics, and can be pressed at high heat settings that would melt synthetic fibers. So many people are quilting today that the selection of cottons designed for quilters is better than it has ever been. Take a bit of time to become familiar with the properties of your fabrics. The knowledge will give you a better understanding of pattern instructions, and it will give you the confidence to make changes when necessary to suit your needs.

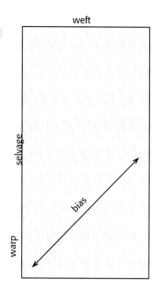

Fabric Grain

Have you ever watched a weaver making fabrics at a loom? The cottons we buy for quilting are made in a similar way. Long threads are stretched on the loom and secured. They are called *warp threads*, and become the lengthwise grain of the fabric. More threads, called *weft threads*, are woven back and forth along the entire length of the warp threads. The weft threads make up the fabric's crosswise grain. Selvages, the bound edges along the sides of fabric, are formed as the weft threads turn to change direction as the weaving process travels down the length of the warp.

Although both grains are referred to as straight-of-grain, the lengthwise grain is less stretchy. Unlike the moving weft threads, warp threads were firmly attached to the loom during the weaving process. The interlaced weft threads help stabilize them. Another stabilizing factor is that there are usually more warp threads than weft threads per square inch (cm). Because of their strength, lengthwise grain strips make excellent stabilizers for quilt borders and sashing.

Cut a small square of fabric and on it on the lengthwise grain (parallel to selvages). Do the same on the crosswise grain, and notice how much more the piece stretches.

Fabric stretches even more on the bias. True bias is defined as a 45° angle to the straight grains, but we refer to any off-grain cut as a bias cut. Tug on your square from corner to corner. It will probably stretch a great deal and may even lose its shape permanently.

To minimize stretch, patch edges on the outer perimeter of a block should be straight grain edges. That is easy to do when cutting squares and rectangles, because their sides are at 90° angles to each other, matching the arrangement of straight grain threads. Triangles all have at least one angled edge, so they also will have at least one bias edge. Analyze triangles to see which edge to cut on the straight grain. Setting triangles are an example of triangles that must be cut in a specific way (see page 146).

A bias edge is sometimes helpful. Stretchy bias strips make it easier to apply binding to quilts with curved edges. They are also used to make thin strips which must be curved to form vines on an appliqué quilt. The edges of other appliqué pieces, such as hearts, are often easier to turn under if cut on the bias.

Fabric Selection

There are no wrong prints. Although they are somewhat more difficult to use for patches in small blocks, even large-scale prints are useful for setting squares or triangles and for borders. When working with large prints, keep finished patch size in mind. Sometimes it's helpful to make a window template (see page 108) of the shape and position it over a print. What you'll see is a preview of how that portion of the fabric would look as that patch. Large prints that change dramatically from area to area sometimes do not look like they were cut from the same piece of fabric. That may or may not be desirable for your quilt, but it is something you should consider.

A useful print type for any quilt, including miniatures, is a print that reads as a solid. From a distance, it may appear to be solid, but on closer inspection you discover a subtle print. These prints can be used to add texture to the quilt when you don't want to introduce clutter.

As you build a fabric collection, try to add fabrics from all color families, even those you don't particularly like. Choose prints of every scale. Do not be afraid to use colors together in ways you never imagined. Look at nature—colors are often combined in ways we do not think of as "matching." Be a good observer, and try to re-create what you see in cloth.

Thread Selection

If you use 100 percent cotton fabrics, we recommend that you sew with 100 percent cotton thread. When thread fibers match the content of fabric, they are less likely to damage patches. Thread that is stronger than cotton, such as polyester, will in time cut through the fabric along seam lines.

Color Value

Stated simply, color value refers to how dark or light a fabric is in relation to others. The amount of contrast between adjoining patches can drastically change the layout of a block or quilt. In *Catching the View* on page 76 lighter strips are used to frame the top and bottom sides of blocks. Altering value gives the quilt a different appearance.

To sort fabrics by value, arrange fabrics you think are of similar value on a wall and stand back. Do any pop out at you? Remove them from the group and check again. Another option is to use a value filter, which masks color, giving you more of a black-and-white image of fabrics. Take care; most of these filters are red, which makes it difficult to judge red fabrics in relation to others.

If you feel intimidated by fabric selection, we recommend you browse the library or quilt shops for a book about color. There are several written specifically for quilters. Visit quilt exhibits to see how others have combined colors.

Fabric Care

We prewash all of our cottons, because we feel the advantages of doing so outweigh the disadvantages. First, all 100 percent cotton shrinks. Cotton is a natural fabric, made from threads spun from fibers of the cotton plant. One characteristic of natural fibers is their tendency to relax, as they attempt to return to their natural state. When cotton fabric is manufactured, threads are stretched on a loom, pulling fibers into an unnaturally straight position. Added coatings help stabilize the threads, keeping them more taut than they want to be. When fabrics are washed, both the agitation of the washing machine and the wicking action of the fibers allow the threads to return to a position more like that in which they grew. Movement in the dryer does the same. Part of what we see as shrinkage is actually the relaxation of the fibers. Fabrics with low thread counts shrink more, because as fibers relax they fill up the larger gaps between threads. If fabrics shrink at different rates, it can create distortions when you launder quilts containing unwashed fabrics.

Second, some dark cottons bleed or lose their dyes, particularly reds and purples. Whether you do or do not plan to prewash, test suspected fabrics to be sure they are colorfast. Submerge a small piece of fabric in soapy water. Let it sit for a while, and then check to see if the water is discolored. Place the wet patch on a white paper towel. Check to see if dye bleeds onto the towel. If the fabric bleeds, try washing it a few times and check again. If the problem continues, do not use the fabric in a quilt. Another option is to purchase a commercial fixing product, such as Retayne, to help set the dye.

Third, quilting cottons arrive from the manufacturer coated with sizing, protectants, and other chemicals. The fabrics have a nice, crisp feel that makes them easy to rotary cut. But if you are sensitive to chemicals, handling coated fabrics or breathing small particles that may flake off of them could cause problems. Prewashing removes most of the loose chemicals. If you prefer to work with a stiffer fabric, use spray starch to add crispness. Yes, that introduces another chemical, but you have the opportunity to read the ingredients list on the can to find out exactly what's in it.

Wash your fabrics in cool water with a mild soap, such as Orvus paste. To help eliminate wrinkles, remove pieces from the dryer before they are completely dry. If you can't press them right away, use clothespins to suspend fabric from hangers.

Pressing Fabrics

The most important thing to remember when using an iron on quilts is the word *press*. That is exactly what you must do—press, letting the weight of the iron do the work for you. Do not move the iron back and forth vigorously across the surface of the fabric. When you must move the iron, take care to do it in a way that does not stretch the block or the quilt.

Quilters disagree on whether or not to use steam in the iron. If you tug at a dampened block, it is more likely to stretch. If fabrics are unwashed, any that bleed may stain surrounding patches when steam dampens them.

We do press, and we prefer to use a dry iron. Pressing opens up the entire width of each seam, which is important when working with small blocks. We think it is important to press as you work and that doing so provides us with a more consistently pieced quilt.

Pressing Basics

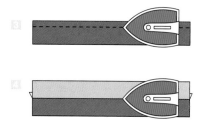

- To press a sewn unit, such as a strip set or a half-square triangle unit, set the iron up and down along the seam on the unopened unit. The fabric on top should be the fabric that the seam allowance will be pressed toward. This helps to set the seam as it was sewn, eliminating puckers. fig. 3

- Lift the top strip up, and place the iron on the underneath strip. Gently work its edge toward and over the seam. Allow its weight to press the seam flat. Move the iron gently up the length of the seam to press the entire length. Turn the unit over and press from the back, moving the iron up and down but not gliding it over the piece. fig. 4

- Press seams in rows before rows are sewn together. Press adjoining seams in opposite directions when possible. The seam allowance pushes upward, forming a slight loft on top of the patch it is pressed under. When lofts meet on opposite sides of adjoining patches, they create seam intersections that butt into each other, making it easy to achieve a perfect match.

■ Use a rotary ruler to make sure each block is square. If a block is distorted, cut a freezer paper square to match its unfinished size. Mark strategic areas of the block, such as the diagonal and the horizontal and vertical centers. Place your block on top of the square and manipulate it to match the square. Do not tug too hard or you will stretch the block more. If a dry iron does not do the job, try using steam or spray starch. Pressing grids are sold commercially and are available in small and large sizes.

■ If you find that straight pins create bunching along the side of units being sewn together, try pressing pieces together for sewing instead. Cottons tend to stick to each other when pressed, so pins are often unnecessary. When you must pin, use long, thin silk pins for smoothest results.

Mother's Fantasy Windows

CHAPTER 3

Rotary Cutting and Template Basics

Rotary cutting is one of the most time-saving skills a quilter can master, because it eliminates the need to mark and cut individual patches of fabric. Not only does rotary cutting speed up quilt assembly, but if done correctly it can enhance accuracy. That is important for small quilts, where even slight deviations in patch sizes can create match-up problems in your blocks. Rotary cutting has eliminated the use of templates for many patterns.

Rotary Cutters

Rotary cutters resemble pizza cutters, with an important difference. Their blades are razor sharp. Many types of cutters are available, all with different handles and protective sheaths. Find one that feels comfortable in your hand. In general, larger blade sizes allow you to cut more layers. This is not as important when working with miniatures, since trying to cut too many layers at one time can lead to inaccuracies. Replace the blade when it no longer makes a swift, clean cut through the cloth. Be sure to keep cutters and blades well out of the reach of children and to retract the safety sheath after each use.

Rotary Mats

Special mats are used for cutting to protect surfaces from the rotary blade and to help the blade stay sharp longer. Most mats are self-healing, meaning that nicks the blade leaves as it passes over the mat are not permanent. Some mats are reversible, with a dark and a light side to contrast with different fabrics. Most mats are marked with a grid, which is an excellent guide to fabric placement but usually not accurate enough to measure strips for cutting. Because they warp, mats should be kept out of direct sunlight and away from heat sources. We recommend you purchase the largest mat you can afford that fits in your work area. Even though your final piece may be small, you often start out with larger pieces of fabric. Large mats make it much easier to cut fabric into strips.

Rotary Rulers

Thick, acrylic, see-through rulers are used to measure strips for cutting. Start with the following basics and add to your collection as you discover what works best for you.

A 6″ × 24″ (15 cm × 60 cm) ruler is indispensable and will enable you to make nearly any type of cut. Make sure it is marked with 30°,

45°, and 60° lines and that dimensions are in ⅛″ (0.3 cm) increments. Thin lines make it easier to determine fabric position.

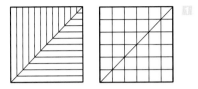

A 6″ × 6″ (15 cm × 15 cm) square is helpful to align and cut
squares and triangle squares. Dimensions are duplicated along two
adjoining sides, with a diagonal guideline running through them.
Marks should be in ⅛″ (0.3 cm) increments.

Shorter rulers are nice for working with fat quarters and fat eighths.
Also useful are 3″-wide (7.5 cm) rulers, since they are less bulky for
making narrow cuts. Specialty rulers help us cut curves and angled edges.
There are hundreds of kinds of rotary rulers. Only you can be the judge of
which ones will be important for your own quilting needs.

Cutting Strips

Patches for most rotary-cut patterns begin as long strips cut from selvage
to selvage on the fabric's crosswise grain. Cutting charts for patterns in
this book indicate how many selvage-to-selvage cuts are required for
rotary cut patches. Before you make the first cut, the fabric must be
folded, and one end must be squared to be an exact 90° angle to the fold.

1. Fold the fabric along its length, selvages together. The bottom fold
    should be straight, with no puckers. Sometimes this means that
    selvages will not be perfectly aligned. Press the piece. If you are
    working on a small mat, you may need to fold the fabric again,
    making it four layers deep. Fold carefully, because each fold creates
    an opportunity for inaccuracies. Strips can also be cut on the
    lengthwise grain, parallel to the selvages.

2. Place the fabric on your rotary mat with the fold near the bottom
    edge of the mat and side to be squared on the left. Align a rotary
    ruler with the folded edge of the fabric, near the left edge. Place a
    long rotary ruler to the left of the first, edges flush against each
    other. Check to make sure lines of both rulers are parallel to the

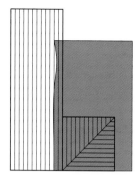

folded edge. (If you are left-handed, work from the opposite end of the fabric, placing rulers in mirror-image positions.) fig. 2

3. Remove the right-side ruler. Place your hand on the long ruler to hold it firmly in place, and roll the rotary cutter from bottom to top directly along its right edge. Spread your fingers out to hold the ruler securely, but take care to keep them out of the path of the cutter. You might need to move your fingers up the ruler as you cut. The fabric edge should now be at a 90° angle to the folded edge. fig. 3

4. Cut required strips from the squared-up edge. For instance, if you must cut 3″ (7.5 cm) strips, align the 3″ (7.5 cm) mark on the ruler with the left edge of the fabric. Align a horizontal line on the bottom of the ruler with the fold. Before each cut make sure that both edges of fabric align with vertical and horizontal markings on the ruler. If they do not, square up the end again before cutting more strips.

✂ *Accuracy Check*

5. Square up one end of a strip and then cut segments from it as needed, aligning the strip with markings on the ruler as required for each shape.

Rotary Helpers

If you find it difficult to cut long strips accurately, work with smaller pieces of fabric until you are accustomed to the technique.

Use spray starch to stiffen fabrics slightly. The crispness helps keep them from distorting under the ruler.

Attach sandpaper tabs to the bottom of rulers to help keep them from slipping on fabric.

Always roll the rotary cutter away from you.

Accuracy Check

Open the strip to its full width and look at the area near the fold. If the strip has a bend in the middle, it means the fabric's left edge was not at a 90° angle to the fold. Check strips periodically to be sure the edge remains square.

You will often see instructions to stack strips for cutting. Be aware that the more strips you stack, the less accurate resulting patches will be. Although it's more time consuming, we prefer to work with no more than two layers.

Using Templates for Pieced Blocks

Templates are exact copies of pieces in a printed pattern. A template is made for each piece in the pattern and then used to mark fabric for cutting. Traditionally, templates were used to mark all pieces, until the advent of the rotary cutter, which revolutionized cutting for quilters. Still, you will find there are times it may be preferable to use traditional template methods. Templates are essential when we need patches with dimensions that cannot be rotary-cut accurately. Targeting a specific area of a print is often easier with a template, because you can select each patch individually and fabric markings can be drawn directly on see-through template material, if necessary. And there are quilters who simply do not like rotary cutters. Many comment that they enjoy the slower-paced motions of making and cutting out each patch.

Making Templates

Templates traditionally are made out of lightweight cardboard. A more durable choice is special template plastic. Many types are available: gridded or plain, transparent or opaque, heat resistant, with two smooth sides or with one slightly rough side that grips fabric. Template plastic is the best choice for pieces you intend to use often. Other traditional options include card stock, posterboard, and sandpaper.

Whether you are making hand-piecing templates or machine-piecing templates, use a fine-tipped pen or pencil to draw them and then cut templates out on the innermost edge of the line. Compare each piece with the original to make sure it is accurate. A fine-tipped marker is important for marking fabric, too. Avoid adding extra width to patches by keeping lines narrow and consistent.

Machine-Piecing Templates

Templates used for machine-piecing include a ¼″ (0.6 cm) seam allowance around all sides of the shape. The most important line is the cutting line. Position these templates right side up on the fabric, and mark around them. Cut out on the line. Match the outer edges for sewing, and sew across the entire width of patches unless a piece must be set-in later (see page 122).

Hand-Piecing Templates

Templates used for hand-piecing generally do not include a seam allowance. The most important line on a hand-piecing template is the seam line. To trace a hand-piecing template, place it face down on the wrong side of the fabric and trace around its edges. The lines are seam lines. Experienced hand sewers estimate a ¼″ (0.6 cm) seam allowance when cutting out the patch. If hand sewing is new to you, we recommend you use a ruler to add ¼″ (0.6 cm) to each side before cutting. Hand-pieced seams do not extend past seam intersections.

Window Templates

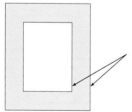

Window templates can be used for hand- or machine-piecing and are helpful for marking pieces that are part of set-in seams (see page 122). A window template is just what its name implies. Trace the shape on template material. Include the seam line and the cutting line. Cut the template out on both lines to expose a window at its center. Marking around the inner edge of the window indicates the seam line, while marks around its outer edge are the cutting line. These versatile templates are a good choice if you wish to target specific areas of fabric. fig. 4

Markings on Templates

Transfer all marks on the original pattern piece to your templates, including grain line and piece number. Other things you might wish to jot down are the number of pieces to cut, if a template must be turned over to cut a reverse image, fabric used, and pattern name. Use any labels that will help you complete the quilt.

Freezer Paper Templates

Using freezer paper to make appliqué templates is described on page 142. It can also be used to make hand- and machine-piecing templates.

1. Position a finished-size template right side down on the nonwaxy side of freezer paper. Trace around it. Trace several copies of each template. Cut out on the lines.

2. Press a template on the wrong side of the fabric. Mark a seam allowance ¼" (0.6 cm) away from each edge and cut out on the marked lines. Leave paper in place. Repeat with additional patches.

3. As you sew patches together, the edges of the paper indicate the seam lines for each piece. This is a handy way to mark and match up patches for set-in seams or to align patches with offset edges. Hand sewers can use the edges of paper as a guide for their seam lines.

Freezer paper templates can often be used several times. Mark and cut more as needed.

Which Way Do We Go?

CHAPTER 4

Basics of Patchwork Shapes

After you have been quilting awhile, you will likely encounter every imaginable shape. The most common are squares, rectangles, and different types of triangles. After reading this chapter, browse through the patterns in *Quick Little Quilts* to see how the different shapes are used. The shapes following are the ones used in *Quick Little Quilts*. These are the most common shapes, particularly for beginning quilters.

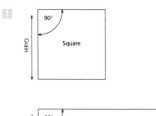

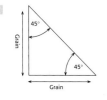

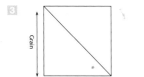

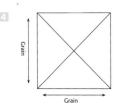

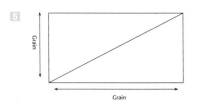

Squares and Rectangles

A *square* is a shape with four right angles and equal sides. A true *rectangle* has four right angles and is twice as long as it is wide. Rectangles of different proportions than this are called *bars*. Squares and rectangles are the easiest patchwork shapes to work with. Their right-angle sides are cut parallel to the fabric's straight grains, stabilizing their edges so that the fabric does not stretch out of shape easily. fig. **1**

Triangles

A *triangle* has three angles and three sides. Since triangles have at least one angled edge, at least one edge is always cut on the fabric's stretchy bias, which makes triangles a little more difficult to work with. fig. **2**

Half-Square Triangles

After squares, the *half-square triangle* is the most frequently used shape in patchwork quilting. It is cut by dividing a square in half once diagonally. The straight grain runs parallel to the triangle's short sides. fig. **3**

Quarter-Square Triangles

The *quarter-square triangle* is cut by dividing a square twice diagonally to form four small triangles. The straight grain is along the longest edge of each. fig. **4**

Long Triangles

A *scalene triangle* has three unequal sides. The variation used most often in quilting is the *right scalene triangle*, known to quilters as the *long triangle*. One angle is 90°. Long triangles are cut by dividing a rectangle or bar diagonally from corner to corner. The straight grain runs parallel to the straight edges. Long triangles are used in *Little Oddfellows Star* on page 22 and *Kittens with the Blues* on page 82. fig. **5**

Seam Allowances for Patchwork Shapes

Unless otherwise stated, piecing templates and dimensions in our cutting charts include a standard ¼" (0.6 cm) seam allowance around each piece. If seams in small blocks add too much bulk, trim them back after sewing.

Working with patchwork shapes is easy once you understand seam allowances. That knowledge gives you a better grasp of how to rotary-cut different shapes. The patches described in this chapter are the ones you will encounter most often when piecing quilts, including the patterns in *Quick Little Quilts*.

Cutting Squares and Rectangles

When a ¼" (0.6 cm) seam allowance is added to a square or rectangle, each side of the finished patch increases by exactly that amount. To rotary-cut squares or rectangles, cut strips along the straight grain that are ½" (1.2 cm) wider than the width of the finished patch, and then cut away segments that are ½" (1.2 cm) longer than the finished width. The sides of the new patch will be parallel to the straight grain. fig. 6

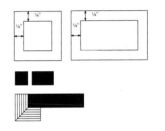

Cutting Triangles

Adding a ¼" (0.6 cm) seam allowance to the angled edges of triangles creates extra seam allowance at their tips. The length of the excess depends on the angle of the triangle. The dimensions of the initial rotary-cut shape depends on how the fabric's straight grain should be positioned.

Cutting Half-Square Triangles

When we add a ¼" (0.6 cm) seam allowance to all sides of a half-square triangle and then connect the legs, there is an excess of ⅜" (0.9 cm) at each angled tip, or a total of ⅞" (2.1 cm) required to compensate for seams on each side. To rotary-cut half-square triangles, cut a square with sides ⅞" (2.1 cm) longer than the finished short sides of the triangle and

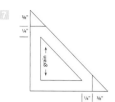

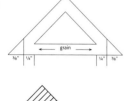

Accuracy Check

Unfinished leg lengths for long triangles are actually just slightly larger than shown but are not a size easily cut with rotary rulers. For small miniatures (blocks under 3" [7.5 cm] square), add 1/16" (0.2 cm) to each seam allowance addition and use accurate rulers to make paper cutting guides for strips and rectangles. Tape them to rotary rulers for easy use. The difference should not create problems with larger blocks.

then cut the square in half once diagonally to produce two triangles with the fabric's straight grain along their short sides. fig. 7

Cutting Quarter-Square Triangles

Quarter-square triangles are cut differently because the straight grain lies parallel to their longest edge. To rotary-cut four of them, cut a square with sides 1¼" (3.1 cm) larger than the finished length of the triangle's longest edge and then cut the square in half twice diagonally. fig. 8

Half- and quarter-square triangles are more difficult than other patchwork shapes to sew accurately, because their bias edges stretch out of shape easily. Beginning on page 115, we have described easy ways to quick-piece two common units the patches are used in.

Cutting Long Triangles

Long triangles can be quick-cut from rectangles. Cut strips ⅝" (1.5 cm) wider than the triangle's finished short side, and then cut rectangular segments that are 1¼" (3.1 cm) longer than the finished long side. Cut rectangles in half once diagonally, depending on the orientation required for the patch's angled edge. fig. 9 ......✂ *Accuracy Check*

If you're ever in doubt about a cut size, draw the finished size of a patch on graph paper, and then surround it with a ¼" (0.6 cm) seam allowance. Mark the fabric grain direction. Study the shape to determine how best to cut it using rotary techniques.

Use your knowledge of seam allowances to help you match up patches for sewing. You will be more aware of how much overlap should occur when aligning sides of differently shaped patches.

Quick-Piecing Half-Square Triangle Units

Two half-square triangles are very often sewn together along their angled edges to make half-square triangle units, called that because each half of the square is occupied by a right, or half-square, triangle. Look at *A Joyous Celebration* on page 10 or *Blazing Baskets* on page 2 to see how these are used.

Half-square triangles are one of the most commonly used patchwork units, and there are several quick-piecing assembly methods. The instructions given here are our two favorites. Both eliminate handling individual triangles, resulting in more accurate units.

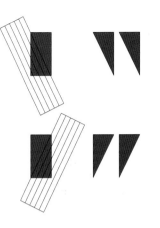

Method 1: Sandwiched Squares

Two squares are sewn together to the right and left of their center diagonal and then cut apart to yield two identical half-square triangle units. It is the best method for creating a group of scrappy triangle squares.

1. Add ⅞″ (2.1 cm) to the finished size of a half-square triangle unit. Use that dimension to cut a square from both fabrics selected for the unit.

2. Use a pencil or permanent marker to draw a diagonal line from corner to corner on the reverse side of the lightest square. fig. 10

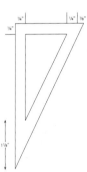

3. Align the marked square with the darker square, right sides together. Sew a seam ¼″ (0.6 cm) from the marked center line. Sew another seam ¼″ (0.6 cm) from the opposite side of the line. If your presser foot cannot gauge an accurate ¼″ (0.6 cm) seam, draw lines on the square before sewing. fig. 11

4. Using scissors or a rotary cutter, cut through both layers on the center line. Open both units, pressing seam allowances toward the dark half, or as directed in the pattern. Trim nubs at seam ends. Units should be exactly ½″ (1.2 cm) longer on each side than the finished size of the triangle square. Repeat to make additional triangle squares. fig. 12 .... ✂ Sewing Tip, page 116

Method 2: Sewing on a Grid

Grid sewing is a good choice if you need many identical half-square triangle units. Draw a grid of squares and then sew two diagonal seams through each. Cut each square apart to produce two triangle squares.

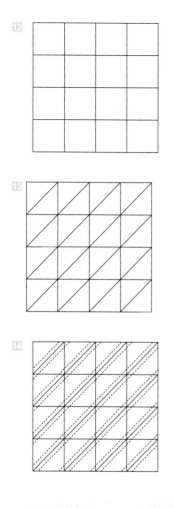

1. Add ⅞″ (2.1 cm) to the finished size of a half-square triangle unit.

2. To determine how many squares to draw in the grid, divide the number of triangle units required by two. Draw the grid on paper and then pin it to fabric before sewing. Leave a margin of approximately ½″ (1.2 cm) around all sides of the grid. Tracing paper pulls away easily after sewing. Plain newsprint and freezer paper are other options. Quilt shops sell freezer paper with graph lines ¼″ (0.6 cm) apart, which makes marking easier. Grids can also be drawn directly on fabric, but fabric can be distorted during the marking process. Even small variations can create problems with miniature blocks.

3. Make a practice grid to construct 32 triangle units that finish at 1″ (2.5 cm) square. Draw 16 1⅞″ (4.6 cm) squares, using a grid of four squares wide and four squares deep to fit on 9″ (22.5 cm) square of fabric. Alter layout to suit the dimensions of your yardage. fig. 12

4. Draw a diagonal line from corner to corner through each square. fig. 13

5. Place triangle unit fabrics right sides together. Press to help them adhere to each other. Center the grid on top of the fabrics and secure it to both with straight pins.

6. Sew a line exactly ¼″ (0.6 cm) from each side of the drawn lines. If your presser foot cannot gauge an accurate ¼″ (0.6 cm) seam, mark sewing lines before beginning. fig. 14

7. Cut triangle squares apart on drawn lines. Remove paper and any stitches that might have overlapped into neighboring units. Press open as in Method 1, trimming nubs from ends of seam allowances. Units should be exactly ½″ (1.2 cm) longer on each side than the finished size of the triangle square.

Accuracy Check

Sewing Tip

Use chain piecing to speed up assembly. Feed a sandwiched pair through the machine, pull it out of the way slightly, and then feed another. Continue until all first seams are sewn. Cut threads between pairs and chain piece again to sew the remaining seams.

Finished size of triangle unit	Grid or square size*	Assembled unit dimensions
1" (2.5 cm)	1⅞" (4.6 cm)	1½" × 1½" (3.7 cm × 3.7 cm)
1½" (3.7 cm)	2⅜" (5.9 cm)	2" × 2" (5 cm × 5 cm)
2" (5 cm)	2⅞" (7.1 cm)	2½" × 2½" (6.2 cm × 6.2 cm)
2½" (6.2 cm)	3⅜" (8.4 cm)	3" × 3" (7.5 cm × 7.5 cm)
3" (7.5 cm)	3⅞" (9.6 cm)	3½" × 3½" (8.7 cm × 8.7 cm)
3½" (8.7 cm)	4⅜" (11 cm)	4" × 4" (10 cm × 10 cm)
4" (10 cm)	4⅞" (12.1 cm)	4½" × 4½" (11.2 cm × 11.2 cm)

*Increase by ⅛" to ¼" (0.3 cm to 0.6 cm) if you prefer to make oversize units, then cut back to enhance accuracy.

Accuracy Check

If your triangle squares are smaller than they should be, try sewing seams with a scant ¼" (0.6 cm) seam allowance. If they are still too small or skewed, we suggest you increase the beginning square or grid size by ⅛" to ¼" (0.3 cm to 0.6 cm) and then use rotary equipment to trim each unit back to its correct size before using it in your quilt. When trimming back, align the 45° line on your rotary ruler with the diagonal seam to make sure each triangle occupies exactly half of the square. There are many rotary rulers available developed specifically for use with triangle squares.

Quick-Piecing Quarter-Square Triangle Units

Make these by using oversized half-square triangle units as their "parents."

1. Determine the finished size of the quarter-square triangle unit and add 1¼" (3.2 cm). Cut one square from two contrasting fabrics.

2. Use half-square triangle Method 1 on page 5 to assemble two half-square triangle units. Each completed unit should be exactly ⅞" (2.1 cm) larger than the finished size of the quarter-square triangle unit.

3. Draw a diagonal line from corner to corner on the reverse side of one triangle square, perpendicular to the seam. Place squares together, dark halves facing lighter halves. Align all edges. fig. 15

4. Sew a seam ¼" (0.6 cm) from each side of the diagonal line, in the same manner as for the parent units. Cut apart on the diagonal line. Press units open and trim nubs at seam allowance. fig. 16

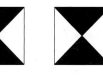

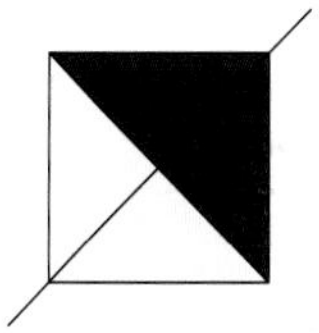

Little Odyfellows Star

CHAPTER 5

Machine-Piecing and Hand-Piecing Basics

Different quilters quilt for different reasons, and any one person may have different objectives from quilt to quilt or even from day to day. For speedy assembly, we usually choose to machine piece. If we need to calm down and relax after a busy day, hand piecing does the trick. Sometimes an oddly shaped set-in piece is much easier to deal with by hand than by machine. Do not be afraid to mix the two techniques if necessary to achieve the design you envision. Understanding the basics of each gives you more assembly options to draw on when you encounter a difficult block.

Machine Piecing Accurate Seams

Before you begin to machine piece, it is important to set up your sewing machine to sew an exact ¼" (0.6 cm) seam, the standard seam allowance used for quilts. Unless you use a method such as foundation piecing (see page 131), exact seams are important and are especially critical for small blocks. A slight difference may not be noticeable in a 12" (30 cm) block but could be enough to keep adjoining units from matching correctly in a 2" (5 cm) block. Test your machine to verify that seams are accurate.

Cut three strips of contrasting fabric, each exactly 1" × 3" (2.5 cm × 7.5 cm). Sew the fabrics together lengthwise using a ¼" (0.6 cm) seam. Press seams toward outer strips. The center strip should be exactly ½" (1.2 cm) wide along its entire length.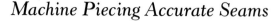

If the strip is too narrow, check to see if the seams were pressed adequately. Make sure a portion of the width is not hidden in the fold of the seam (see "Pressing Fabric," page 100). Also check to be sure that strip edges align accurately along their entire width. Strips may have shifted during sewing. If the strip is too wide, check the edges for exact alignment, and make sure strips were cut the correct width.

If pressing is adequate and edges are aligned, you need to adjust the way you gauge a ¼" (0.6 cm) seam. Cut several more 1" (2.5 cm) strips of fabric to use in test units. Sew a new set and measure carefully after each change to your machine setup.

- If you are using a ¼" (0.6 cm) presser foot, adjustment might be a simple matter of gauging where the fabric moves under the foot. If you've always sewn with patch edges aligned flush with the foot's right side, try feeding them through so that edges are just slightly left of that spot, to shorten the seam allowance. Shift the opposite direction if you must increase the allowance.

- Try changing needle position.

If seams are still not accurate, mark a sewing guide directly on the machine's throatplate.

1. Position a strip of ¼″ (0.6 cm) graph paper under your presser foot. Drop the needle directly on a line of the paper, leaving one ¼″ (0.6 cm) grid to its right. Drop the presser foot, making sure its edges are parallel to marked lines. Align a piece of masking tape with the paper's right edge.

2. Sew a test set and check strip measurement again. If not accurate, shift tape to the right or left and keep testing until you are sewing an accurate ¼″ (0.6 cm) seam.

3. Once the correct position is established, apply several more pieces of masking tape over the first to form a better guide for fabric. Other guide options include moleskin or purchasing a commercial guide, usually an adhesive-backed strip of thick plastic.

You might be tempted to think inaccurate seams will not matter—that if all seams are the same it will not create a problem, as in simple Nine-Patch blocks. fig. 2 But what if different types of blocks must join, such as the Snowball and Star blocks used in *A Joyous Celebration* on page 10? The Snowballs have only two sewn seams on each side. The Star blocks have six, including seams within half-square triangle units. If each seam is off by ¹⁄₃₂″ (0.1 cm), there will be a difference of ⅛″ (0.3 cm) along the side of the block, which can create matchup problems in small quilts. A ¹⁄₁₆″ (0.2 cm) seam variation would result in a ¼″ (0.6 cm) difference. fig. 3

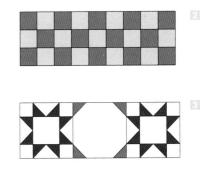

Scant Seams

When you have adjusted seam width, it will likely be what we call a "scant" ¼″ (0.6 cm) seam. Rotary-cut pieces are usually slightly different than their template-cut counterparts, due to the absence of marked lines. If you piece a template-cut quilt, you may need to adjust the seam allowance slightly to compensate for the slight extra width of patches.

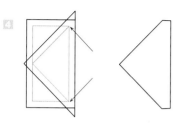

Sewing Patches Together

Patches are positioned right sides together for sewing, with edges of like shapes exactly aligned. When a triangle is sewn to a square, at least one end of the triangle overlaps an edge of the square, due to an excess of seam allowance at triangle tips. To match unlike shapes, remember that the finished seam of each patch will still match exactly. If you are ever in doubt, measure inward ¼″ (0.6 cm) to mark seam intersections, then match those intersections for sewing. Sew across the entire width of patches unless a patch must be set-in to the area later. No backstitches are necessary. fig. 4

✂ Nubbing Triangle Tips

Nubbing Triangle Tips

Nubbing guides are helpful when you must sew many angled edges to a square or rectangle. Make a paper template of both shapes involved, marking finished seams and cut edges. Position templates right sides together, as if they were fabric, aligning the ends of finished seams exactly. Trim the triangle tips to match the outer edges of the square or rectangle. Tape the guide to a rotary ruler. Align it with each triangle to remove fabric tips that extend past its edges. Edges can now be matched exactly for sewing.

Assembling a Block

Blocks are usually assembled by first joining individual patches in rows and then sewing rows together. When possible, seam allowances in adjoining rows are pressed in opposite directions. This creates a slight loft on the front of each seam. When opposing lofts are butted together it is easy to achieve a perfect match at intersections. Strip piecing (see page 127) eliminates the need to cut and sew individual patches. fig. 5

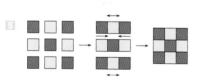

Chain Piecing

Use this time-saver to sew together individual pieces or even when assembling rows of a block. Feed a matched unit through the machine, but instead of cutting the threads, continue feeding units under the presser foot. When finished, clip threads between units and press.

Setting-In

Some blocks cannot be assembled by sewing rows together with continuous seams. Instead, pieces must be set-in to an opening left by previously joined patches. Bow Tie is one example. fig. 6

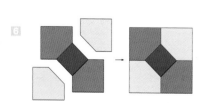

The most important thing to remember about set-in patches is that seams never extend into seam allowances. If you mark intersections on patches before beginning, you will find that setting-in is an easy task.

1. Construct a template (see page 107) of the reverse side of each shape that borders the set-in seam. Include seam allowances. Mark seam lines on each template. Use an awl or other sharp object to make a hole in the template at each seam intersection involved in the setting-in process. Holes should be very small. If they are too large, it will be difficult to tell exactly where seams meet. fig. 7

    If you feel more comfortable viewing the entire seam as you match and sew, make a window template (see page 108). Align its edges with the outer edge of the patch, and mark around the inside opening on sides involved in setting-in. fig. 8

2. Align a template with the reverse side of a patch. Insert a pencil tip through each hole to mark intersections. Use a white or yellow pencil or a chalk or soapstone marker on dark fabrics.

3. Align a Bow Tie patch with one side of the center patch, right sides together. Match seam intersections at each end, securing with pins. Sew a line from dot to dot, backstitching at each end for stability. Do not sew into the seam allowance. fig. 9

4. Use the same technique to sew a Bow Tie patch to the opposite side of the center square.

5. Set-in a background patch. Align a background patch to the center square. When seams are matched, intersection dots should be directly over the seam lines of patches below. Sew the patch to the piece, backstitching at beginning and end. Do not sew past the seam intersection. Remove unit from the machine. fig. 10

6. Pin an edge of the background to the adjoining edge of a Bow Tie piece, matching seam intersections where previous seam ended.

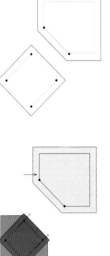

Begin sewing at the spot where previous seam ended, backstitching to add stability. Continue sewing to the end of the patches, since that edge does not involve set-in pieces. Repeat to attach the opposite side of the background to the adjoining Bow Tie patch.

7. Add the background piece to the opposite side using the method in Steps 5 and 6.

For more ways to set-in patches, see *Catching the View*, page 77; *Medallion Star*, page 45; and *Mother's Fantasy Windows*, page 53.

Hand Piecing

Although quick piecing has grown in popularity over the years, many quilters still enjoy the quiet relaxation that hand piecing can provide.

Adapting Patterns for Hand Piecing

The patterns in *Quick Little Quilts* assume you are machine piecing, but it is easy to convert them to hand piecing. See page 108 for more information about hand-piecing templates.

- Use the patch sizes listed in cutting charts to make templates, and then mark inward ¼" (0.6 cm) on each side. Trim on both lines to make window templates.

- Finished size patches are included on patterns for all foundation-pieced blocks, making them easy to trace on template plastic.

- Patch sizes may not be as easy to determine for strip-pieced blocks. Use graph paper to draw the finished block. Cut out the pieces and glue them to template material, or trace them on template plastic.

- Assemble blocks in a similar manner as for machine piecing. Sew units in rows together first, and then sew the rows together. It's not necessary to press until the quilt is complete.

Piecing by Hand

Many hand piecers prefer to use *sharps*, the thin needles used for appliqué. Thread your needle with about 20″ (50 cm) of good-quality cotton thread. Gray thread blends easily with most prints.

1. Place two patches to be joined right sides together with seam lines aligned. Connect seam ends by stabbing a pin through each, traveling through both layers. Add pins along the length of the seam if necessary. fig. 12

2. Remove the pin on one end and insert the needle through the same hole. Some people like to use a knot at the end of the thread. Others prefer to leave a 1″ (2.5 cm) tail at the beginning, and take a few backstitches to secure the thread. fig. 13

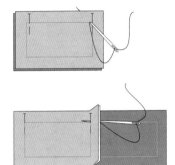

3. Use a small running stitch to sew the length of the seam. Do not sew past the seam intersection. Take a backstitch every inch (2.5 cm) or so to add stability. Check the back side of the piece often to make sure the seam stays on that patch's marked seam line.

4. When you reach the end of the patch, stop sewing and backstitch. Sew remaining pieces to the row, and then assemble all rows.

5. Sew rows together. Match and pin all seam ends as in Step 1, adding pins as necessary to keep seams in both units aligned along the length of the row. Backstitch when you reach a seam allowance. Insert the needle through base of the allowance, coming out on the opposite side. Take a stitch, then a backstitch. Sew to the end of the row, leaving all seam allowances unsewn. Join all rows. fig. 14

6. Sew blocks together in a similar manner, leaving seam allowances free. Press when the quilt top is completely assembled.

Carolina Byways variation

CHAPTER 6

Strip-Piecing Basics

Strip piecing is a time-saving technique that eliminates cutting and sewing together individual pieces of fabric. Long strips of fabric are sewn together, pressed, and then cut into segments that replace a block or portion of a block. *Carolina Byways* on page 126 is entirely strip pieced. The technique is helpful any time it is acceptable to use identical segments within a quilt. Even scrappy quilts can be made using strip-piecing techniques, by shortening the length of strips used, thus reducing the number of identical segments. Like other quick-piecing methods, strip piecing eliminates the need to handle individual pieces of fabric. If strips are cut and sewn together carefully, the technique can enhance the accuracy of any quilt, especially miniatures, whose tiny patches easily stretch or fray with too much handling.

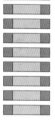

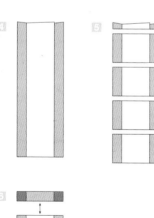

Quick Piecing a Puss-in-a-Corner Block

This variation of the traditional Puss-in-a-Corner block can be entirely strip pieced. Follow the instructions below to make eight 2½″ (6 cm) blocks. Sew them together in a setting of your choice or as shown.

Even though units are small, these little blocks are easy to make if you cut and align strips carefully and sew an exact ¼″ (0.6 cm) seam allowance. If you have not verified your seam accuracy, follow the instructions on page 120 before sewing the strips together.

1. Determine the desired size for each unit within a block. This block can be divided into a grid of five squares across and five squares down, so it is called a Five-Patch block (see page 168). If the units each finish at ½″ (1.2 cm), the block will measure 2½″ (6 cm) square.

2. Cut two dark corner strips, each 1″ × 9″ (2.5 cm × 22 cm). Cut one medium inner strip, 2″ × 9″ (2.5 cm × 22 cm).

   ·······✂ *Accuracy Check*

3. Sew a narrow dark strip lengthwise to each side of the wider light strip. Press seams toward the dark strips.

4. Use your rotary-cutting equipment to square up one end of the strip set and then cut eight 1″-wide (2.5 cm) segments from it.

5. Cut two medium strips for the second strip set, each 1″ × 9″ (2.5 cm × 22 cm). Cut one light strip, 2″ × 9″ (5 cm × 22 cm).

6. Sew a medium narrow strip lengthwise to each side of the wider light strip. Press seams toward the medium strip.

7. Use your rotary-cutting equipment to square up one end of the strip set and then cut four 2″ (5 cm) segments from it.

8. Sew narrow segments from the first strip set to the top and bottom of a wider segment from the second strip set to complete the block. fig. 6

Tips for Successful Strip Piecing

- If you have problems cutting and sewing long strips accurately, use shorter strips. Make additional strip sets to compensate for the reduced length.

- Press edges together when aligning them for sewing. Cottons tend to stick to each other, helping retain alignment as the seam is sewn. Pins are often unnecessary.

- Use spray starch to stiffen fabrics slightly, making it easier to cut accurately.

- Press strip sets carefully but thoroughly so that no patch width is "hidden" in a seam. See "Pressing Fabrics" on page 99.

Accuracy Check

To determine the cut length of segments, add ½" (1.2 cm) for seam allowances to the finished length of each segment. Then use this formula to determine strip length.

Cut segment length × # of cuts per block × # of blocks + ½" (1.2 cm) for squaring up = length required

Stretching to the Stars variation

CHAPTER 7

Foundation-Piecing Basics

Foundation piecing is a traditional technique that has grown in popularity in recent years, with miniature quilt enthusiasts among the first to recognize its potential for producing accurate blocks. With foundation piecing, an exact replica, or *template*, is drawn of all or a portion of a block. No seam allowances are included, except the one around the outer perimeter of the unit. All pieces are sewn directly to the template, with seams staying on marked lines.

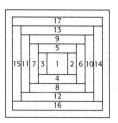

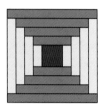

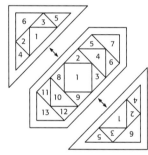

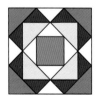

For the method used in this book, fabric is positioned on the reverse side of the foundation template, with raw edges overlapping drawn lines. When seams are sewn on the front side, directly on the lines, the overlapped edges become seam allowances. If you position fabric correctly and are careful to sew on the lines, your blocks will be perfect every time, no matter how small the patches are.

Foundation piecing is possible when the layout is such that one patch is added to an entire side of a block. Log Cabin blocks are a good example. Piecing begins in the center of the block, as shown in our Courthouse Steps variation on page 71, and continues outward in numerical order. Each new log is stitched across the entire length or width of earlier patches. fig. 1

Sometimes it is not possible to foundation piece a block as one unit, but the accuracy that can be achieved using foundations is good motivation to use it for segment piecing. The block shown here is foundation pieced in segments, and then segments are sewn together to complete the block. It would have been much more difficult to sew accurate miniature blocks if we had chosen to piece it using traditional patch-to-patch techniques. As you become more accustomed to this method, you will find you begin to look more carefully at quilt blocks to assess their foundation-piecing potential. fig. 2

Foundation Materials

Permanent foundations are made from materials such as muslin and remain in the quilt forever. We prefer not to use permanent foundations for quilts because they add an extra layer, making it more difficult to hand-quilt the piece. Keep in mind that muslin, the most commonly used permanent material, sometimes has a tendency to stretch out of shape as blocks are assembled, which can result in skewed blocks. Nonwoven interfacing is a better choice for permanent foundations.

Temporary foundations are removed from blocks before the quilt is sandwiched with batting and backing. Very smooth tracing paper is our first choice for temporary foundations. It remains stable as the block is assembled but tears away easily when sewing is complete, without pulling out or distorting stitches. It is easy to see marked lines from the reverse side of tracing paper, which leads to faster and more accurate patch placement. Visible lines allow us to use smaller patches, because we have a clear view of where our seams will be. Another advantage of tracing paper is that fabrics stick to it slightly when pressed, which helps keep fabrics from shifting as new patches are added.

Plain newsprint is another option for temporary foundations. It is available in pads at most office supply stores. It is easier to remove than heavier bond papers. Tissue paper works fine for blocks with few pieces. It is easy to remove but sometimes tends to tear away before you want it to.

A product called Easy Tear is available commercially. It is a nonwoven material that remains stable as you assemble blocks and is easy to remove when sewing is complete.

Making Foundation Templates

Think of foundation templates as sewing blueprints. They are your guide to block assembly, and they are the one aspect of the foundation method where accurate marking is essential. If the image is drawn incorrectly, your blocks will not be accurate. Mechanical pencils or fine-tipped permanent markers help you draw accurate lines. Regular pencils should be sharpened often to keep lines consistent. Always use a straightedge as a guide, making sure to position it so that lines match those on the template exactly. Flexible curves can be used as a guide for curved templates. There are several ways to transfer images to foundations.

- Trace each image individually.

- Draw the image on paper with a hot-iron transfer pen, and then use the master to transfer the shape onto tracing paper. When the image no longer transfers, draw over lines again with the fine-tip pen. Make sure the second set of lines matches the first exactly.

- Trace the image on one sheet of paper. Stack several sheets of tracing paper under the drawing and hold all sheets together with staples or paper clips. Use an unthreaded needle to machine-sew through all marked lines. Follow the punched lines when positioning and sewing patches. Experiment with stitch length and needle sizes. The holes should form an easy-to-follow line, but don't make them so close together that paper falls away during assembly.

- Stack foundation material, alternating it with carbon paper. Place the original on top and secure all layers. Use a seamstress's tracing wheel to transfer the image to foundations below. Make sure the wheel rolls directly on marked lines. The number of copies you can make at one time will depend on the thickness of your foundations.

- If you are careful, photocopies can be used. Choose a high-quality copier, and make sure it is set to reproduce at exactly 100 percent. Position the original template near the center of the copier's image area, and make sure it is laying perfectly flat. Before sewing, check the dimensions of each copy with a ruler, and compare it with the original template.

- Use a computer program to reproduce images, or scan templates at 100 percent. Print images on a laser printer. If you have an ink-jet printer, make sure to use a dry iron: inks could bleed onto fabric.

Be sure to transfer all numerical markings, too. In addition, mark fabric designations on each piece. Since we are sewing on the reverse side of a template, you must always remember that the block will be a mirror image of the printed side. Jotting down a short notation on each area, such as "dark" or "light," will keep the layout accurate as you work.

Fabric Grain

When we assemble a block, we try to minimize stretch by making sure that fabric on the outer edges is cut on the straight grain. Another way to prevent stretch is to sew bias edges to straight grain edges when possible. Even though we sometimes use odd-sized scraps for the foundation method, we should still keep those goals in mind. Our patterns all include recommended patch sizes and cutting instructions for them. Once you have mastered foundation piecing, you might wish to use smaller patches.

Stitch Length

Stitches should be shorter than normal, but length will vary depending on the project and the type of foundation material used. Very short seams, such as those in our dollhouse miniatures, must usually be sewn with a shorter stitch length than long seams in a 6″-square (15 cm) block. Fourteen to 20 stitches per inch (5.5 to 8 stitches per cm) is the normal range. In general, stitches should be short enough to remain stable when foundations are pulled away but not so short that they cause bunching or unnecessary wear on the fabric or are impossible to remove if a seam must be resewn.

Needle Size

A smaller needle that leaves smaller tracks in the fabric is more appropriate to the delicate scale of a very tiny block.

Foundation Piecing a Flying Geese Strip

The following instructions will lead you step-by-step in piecing a four-part strip of Flying Geese. This geese strip includes a ¼″ (0.6 cm) seam allowance around all outer edges.

1. Cut two squares from Flying Geese fabric, using the size given in the pattern you are using. If you are just practicing, use the sizes given for the Flying Geese pieced border on page 34. Cut each square in half once diagonally to produce two right triangles. Because seam allowances are estimated, patches need not be cut to exact sizes as for most other piecing methods.

2. Cut four squares from background fabric. Cut each square in half once diagonally as in Step 1, to produce eight triangles with the straight grain on their short edges.

......✂ Sewing Tip

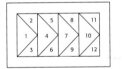

Sewing Tip

Many quilt shops sell a wooden "iron," strips of smooth wood with a spatula-like end that make it easy to press foundation patches in place.

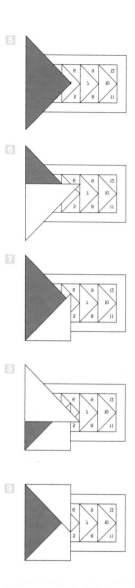

3. Place a Flying Geese triangle right side up on the reverse side of the foundation, centering it over the image of Piece 1. Secure with a pin, or press lightly to adhere triangle to tracing paper. The first piece is the only piece positioned right side up, all other pieces are placed right side down for sewing. fig. 5

4. Turn the foundation over, printed side facing you. You should be able to see the shadow of the fabric triangle. Does it overlap all lines that surround Piece 1? Is the overlap enough to create a stable seam allowance when those lines are sewn? Does the bottom edge of the triangle extend past the outermost line of the template?

5. Position a background triangle right side down and centered along a short edge of the Flying Geese triangle. Hold both fabrics in place and flip to the front side of the foundation. Sew directly on the line separating the two triangles, beginning and ending the seam two or three stitches on either side of the line. fig. 6

6. Flip the background triangle right side up. Hold the foundation up, printed side facing you. Check shadows to make sure the edges of Piece 2 overlap all drawn lines around its perimeter, including the outermost seam allowance line on the foundation's perimeter. Trim back seam allowance if necessary to reduce bulk, and then press (or finger-press) in place. fig. 7

✄ Sewing Tip

7. Center a second background triangle right side down along the opposite edge of the large triangle. Hold in place and flip to the front side of the foundation. Sew on the line separating the two triangles, beginning and ending the seam two or three stitches on either side of the line. fig. 8

8. Remove block from the sewing machine and flip the new triangle right side up. Check placement as before. If correct, trim back seam allowance if necessary and press triangle in place. fig. 9

Sewing Tip

When trimming back seam allowances, always trim through all layers. Otherwise your block will end up with a bulky mass of uneven edges on its reverse side.

9. Position a large Flying Geese triangle right side down on top of previous patches. Use the V formed where background triangles meet to guide placement. The long edge of the new triangle should be centered at the tip of the V and overlap it by approximately ¼″ (0.6 cm). fig.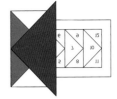

10. Flip the foundation over and sew on the long horizontal line separating the large triangle from the first two small background triangles, beginning and ending a few stitches on either side of the line. Remove from the machine. Look at the front of your foundation, and notice that seams intersect each other. This continues as all new patches are added and helps add stability to the piece. fig.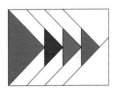

11. Flip the new triangle right side up and check placement as before. Trim back excess seam allowance, including the tip of the first large triangle, which usually extends into it. Press in place.

 Sewing Tip

12. Add all remaining triangles in the same manner, checking placement and trimming excess seam allowances after each addition. After the final triangle is sewn, press the block.

13. Trim the foundation on the outer edge of the outermost line. The strip is now ready to use and includes a seam allowance around its outer perimeter. fig.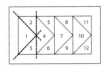

Assembling the Quilt

Some foundation-pieced blocks have bulky seam allowances along their outer edges, which can make it difficult to match intersections when blocks are joined. Stab a straight pin through areas where blocks should meet, such as the points of triangles. Pull pins taut as you sew toward them, to keep fabrics from shifting.

Remove foundations from seam allowances as you join blocks. We recommend you leave remaining foundations in place until borders are added, or for quilts with no borders, until all blocks are sewn together.

Sewing Tip

Do not worry too much about placing patches exactly as we have shown. Part of the fun of foundation piecing is that you are free to estimate, and you do have a bit of extra seam allowance for flexibility. Our instructions are guidelines to help you visualize placement.

Medallion Star

CHAPTER 8

Appliqué Basics

Appliqué is the process of sewing one or more smaller pieces of fabric onto a larger background. *Quick Little Quilts* has two projects that combine piecing and appliqué, *Pitchers for Tildy's Cabin* on page 69 and *Catching the View* on page 77. Both contain appliqué shapes with gentle curves—easy for quilters of all skill levels.

There are many ways to prepare pieces for appliqué. This chapter details two popular methods. The first is *needleturn appliqué*, in which pieces are pinned to the background fabric, but edges are not turned under until the pieces are actually sewn in place. The second is *freezer paper appliqué*, in which patches are prepared by turning the edges under and pressing them onto the waxy side of freezer paper shapes. Edges stay in place while you appliqué around each piece.

Making Templates

Appliqué templates do not contain seam allowances. We suggest you trace shapes on clear or opaque template plastic. Some types are heat resistant, which allows you to press seam allowances around their edges. Plastic templates are durable and give you a good view of the fabric you are marking.

Use a photocopier to enlarge appliqué templates. Any small distortion that does take place is usually not noticeable. Make copies of full-sized patterns and glue them to plastic, lightweight cardboard, or sandpaper. Cut out each shape to complete the template. Photocopiers are also useful for enlarging or reducing patterns.

Although they are used in different ways for different appliqué methods, you will need a template for each shape in an appliqué project.

Preparing the Background

For simple appliqué layouts, such as our Pitcher block in *Pitchers for Tildy's Cabin* on page 69, fold and finger-press the background piece vertically, horizontally, and along its diagonals. Resulting creases are your guide to the block's center and equally spaced areas surrounding it. Use them to help position pieces. For more complicated blocks, use a light table to mark each piece's position directly on the fabric.

There is no need to turn under seam allowances on edges that will be hidden under another piece. If you prefer to secure the raw edges, use a running stitch to sew them to the background.

Working with Curves

Inside (concave) curves, such as the top edge of our Pitcher, fold under more easily when clipped. Use sharp-tipped scissors to make tiny clips perpendicular to the seam allowance. Do not clip all the way to the fold line. Clips are not necessary for outside (convex) curves. fig. 1

Perfect Points

Trim excess seam allowance from points, such as the tip of the cat's tail shown here. Turn under along the entire side of cat's tail as instructed for the appliqué method used. If the seam allowance at the folded-under tip still extends past the allowance on opposite side of tail, trim it back a bit more. Fold under opposite side of tail to continue. fig. **2**

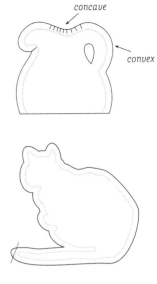

Needleturn Appliqué

In needleturn appliqué, raw edges are turned under as you sew.

1. Make a template for each different shape in your project. Position a template on the right side of fabric and trace around it with a pencil or fine-tipped permanent marker.

2. Cut out the piece, adding a ³⁄₁₆″ (0.4 cm) seam allowance around all sides. Repeat Steps 1 and 2 for all pieces in the design. Trim points and clip curves if necessary.

3. Pin or baste pieces to the background fabric, adding them from the rear forward, depending on their position in the design.

4. Appliqué the rear piece. Use matching thread in a slender needle, such as a *sharp* or milliners' needle. Knot the thread and bring the needle up through the marked fold line of the piece.

5. Use the tip of the needle to fold under the seam allowance a short distance in front of the insertion point, encasing the knot in the fold. Make sure the marked line isn't visible. Use your fingers to hold the fold in place.

6. Insert the needle into the background fabric right next to where it came through the patch. Move the tip of the needle up through the background again, approximately ¹⁄₁₆″ (0.2 cm) from where it was

Seam Allowances

Unless you are using a thin, loosely woven cloth, appliqué seam allowances generally do not need to be ¹⁄₄″ (0.6 cm) wide. Start out with a ³⁄₁₆″ (0.4 cm) seam allowance or slightly less. Trim back if you feel the seam is too bulky.

inserted, catching a few threads of the appliqué piece as it returns. Insert into the background again, and take another short stitch. Tug each stitch slightly to help hide threads.

7. Continue sewing around the shape, folding under only short lengths of the seam allowance at a time, until edges are secure. If you find it difficult to fold under edges with the needle, try guiding fabric with a toothpick.

8. After the final stitch, insert needle through the background fabric. Take a small stitch behind the patch, leaving a small loop. Insert the needle and thread through the loop and pull to tie off thread. Clip excess tail of thread. Appliqué remaining pieces to the background, working forward.

Freezer Paper Appliqué

Freezer paper appliqué uses freezer paper to baste under seam allowances before pieces are added to the background.

1. Trace around a right-side-up template on the nonwaxy side of freezer paper. Cut out piece on the line. Repeat, cutting the total number of pieces required for each template in your design.

2. Use a hot iron to press the waxy side of freezer paper shapes to the front side of fabric. Cut out each shape, adding an approximate ³⁄₁₆″ (0.4 cm) seam allowance around all edges.

3. Peel off freezer paper and center it on the wrong side of the shape, waxy side up. Use a straight pin to secure it to the patch. Trim points and clip curves if necessary. Repeat for all pieces.

4. Use the tip of a hot, dry iron to press the seam allowance over the edges of each freezer paper shape. Fabric will adhere to the paper's softened coating. This step takes the place of basting under, or turning as you go in the needleturn method.

........✂ Sewing Tip

Sewing Tip

Avoid burned fingers by using a toothpick or other non-heat-conducting object, to help fold under edges. Finger wraps are available commercially and are a handy tool to have if you plan to appliqué often.

5. Arrange pieces on the block as for the needleturn method, and then appliqué. Try to avoid stitching through the freezer paper.

6. When you near the last few inches of the design, use your fingers or tweezers to pull away freezer paper. The seam should refold easily. Another option is to stitch around each piece, and then use sharp scissors to make a slit through the background fabric. Remove paper through the opening.

7. Tie off threads as for needleturn appliqué.

Sewing Tip

Sewing Tip

No matter which method you use, spray starch helps tackle unruly edges. Spray a bit in the can's lid, and use cotton-tipped sticks to apply it to edges. Press under.

Pitchers for Tildy's Cabin

CHAPTER 9

Settings and Borders

A quilt *setting* or *set* describes the way blocks are arranged in the quilt. Most blocks take on a different look when their orientation is changed. Adding the borders is the final stage of making the quilt top, framing the blocks within the setting. Browse through the patterns to view the different layouts, keeping in mind as you do that blocks from any pattern can be arranged in any of the settings. Size differences may mean you need to recalculate dimensions for surrounding pieces.

Straight Sets

Straight-set blocks can be arranged side by side or can be alternated with another block. The quilt top from *Little Oddfellows Star* on page 23 changes dramatically if only one of the blocks is used. To assemble a straight-set quilt, sew blocks in horizontal rows and then sew rows together. Seams are easier to match if seam allowances in adjoining rows are pressed in opposite directions. fig. 1

Plain squares, called *setting squares*, can be used to replace one of the original blocks. Setting squares are equal to the unfinished size of the block they will be sewn next to. Snowballs and other simple blocks are often used as alternates because they link with the design in the main block to create a continuous flow of lines across the quilt's surface. fig. 2

Set-on-Point

The quilt's character changes if blocks are placed on-point. fig. 3 As with straight-set quilts, on-point blocks can be sewn next to setting squares or alternate blocks. Using setting squares between pieced blocks in any quilt is an easy way to increase quilt size without piecing additional blocks.

Components in on-point quilts are sewn together in diagonal rows, with setting triangles and corner triangles sewn to the ends of rows to fill in the jagged outer edges. They can be plain fabric, as shown here, or pieced, as in the quilt *Pitchers for Tildy's Cabin* on page 68. Diagonal rows are joined to complete the quilt top. fig. 4

Setting and Corner Triangles

Setting and corner triangles can be cut from rotary-cut squares of fabric, but two different methods must be used. Quilts are less stretchy when patches are positioned so that the straight grain lies parallel to their outer perimeter, so the method we use to cut triangles depends on which sides of the patch we want the straight grain to lie on.

Cutting Setting Triangles

Setting triangles are cut with the straight grain on their long edges. Cut a straight grain square twice diagonally to produce four. fig. 5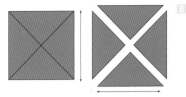

To determine the necessary beginning square size, use a two-part formula. Find the finished diagonal size of the blocks in the quilt, and then add a seam allowance to that figure. Round the answer up to the nearest $\frac{1}{8}''$ (0.1 cm).

> **Finished block size × 1.41 = Finished diagonal**
>
> **Finished diagonal + 1.25 = Size of square**

Cutting Corner Triangles

Corner triangles are cut with the straight grain along their short edges. Cut a square with straight grain sides in half once diagonally to produce two corner triangles. fig. 6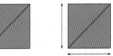

To determine beginning square size, use the following formula, rounding the answer up to the nearest $\frac{1}{8}''$ (0.1 cm).

$$\frac{\text{Finished diagonal}}{2} + 0.875''\ (2.1\ cm) = \text{Square size}$$

Sashing

Blocks can be surrounded by plain or pieced sashing, which is fabric strips used to separate blocks from each other. *Stretching to the Stars*, on page 16, contains an example of pieced sashing. Pieced segments are sewn to each side of the block, with smaller blocks added at the corners. Star blocks in the variation of that quilt, shown on page 130, are surrounded by plain strips of sashing, often called *simple* or *continuous sashing*.

Cutting Chart for Setting Pieces

Block size	Setting squares	Squares for setting triangles	Squares for corner triangles
1″ × 1″ 2.5 cm × 2.5 cm	1½″ × 1½″ 3.7 cm × 3.7 cm	2¾″ × 2¾″ 6.8 cm × 6.8 cm	1⅝″ × 1⅝″ 3.9 cm × 3.9 cm
2″ × 2″ 5 cm × 5 cm	2½″ × 2½″ 6.2 cm × 6.2 cm	4⅛″ × 4⅛″ 10.3 cm × 10.3 cm	2⅜″ × 2⅜″ 5.6 cm × 5.6 cm
3″ × 3″ 7.5 cm × 7.5 cm	3½″ × 3½″ 8.7 cm × 8.7 cm	5½″ × 5½″ 13.8 cm × 13.8 cm	3″ × 3″ 7.4 cm × 7.4 cm
4″ × 4″ 10 cm × 10 cm	4½″ × 4½″ 11.2 cm × 11.2 cm	7″ × 7″ 17.3 cm × 17.3 cm	3¾″ × 3¾″ 9.2 cm × 9.2 cm
5″ × 5″ 12.5 cm × 12.5 cm	5½″ × 5½″ 13.7 cm × 13.7 cm	8⅜″ × 8⅜″ 20.8 cm × 20.8 cm	4½″ × 4½″ 10.9 cm × 10.9 cm
6″ × 6″ 15 cm × 15 cm	6½″ × 6½″ 16.2 cm × 16.2 cm	9¾″ × 9¾″ 24.4 cm × 24.4 cm	5⅛″ × 5⅛″ 12.7 cm × 12.7 cm
7″ × 7″ 17.5 cm × 17.5 cm	7½″ × 7½″ 18.7 cm × 18.7 cm	11⅛″ × 11⅛″ 27.9 cm × 27.9 cm	5⅞″ × 5⅞″ 14.4 cm × 14.4 cm
8″ × 8″ 20 cm × 20 cm	8½″ × 8½″ 21.1 cm × 21.2 cm	12⅝″ × 12⅝″ 31.4 cm × 31.4 cm	6⅝″ × 6⅝″ 16.2 cm × 16.2 cm
9″ × 9″ 22.5 cm × 22.5 cm	9½″ × 9½″ 23.7 cm × 23.7 cm	14″ × 14″ 35 cm × 35 cm	7¼″ × 7¼″ 18 cm × 18 cm

Accuracy Check

We often cut setting and corner triangles larger than necessary and then trim back to square up edges after the quilt top is complete.

1. Add ½″ (1.2 cm) to the desired finished width. Cut long strips that width. It is usually best to cut all strips along the lengthwise grain, which is less stretchy than the crosswise grain. If you are using a directional fabric, it might be necessary to cut vertical and horizontal strips along different grains.

2. Cut segments for the short, vertical pieces that go between blocks. Each segment should be cut to match the length of an unfinished block. For instance, if your blocks finish at 3″ × 3″ (7.5 cm × 7.5 cm), strips should be 3½″ (8.7 cm) long.

3. Sew a short sashing strip between adjoining blocks. Add them using the same technique as for straight-sewn borders, described on page 150. Repeat for all rows. fig. 7

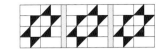

4. Determine how long horizontal strips should be. Multiply the finished width of the blocks in each row by the number of blocks, and add the finished width of each vertical sashing. To that add ½" (1.2 cm) to allow for seams.

5. Use the length calculated in Step 4 to cut the required number of horizontal strips. You'll need a strip to sew between each row and strips for the top and bottom. To help match blocks from row to row, use your rotary ruler to make marks along the sashing to correspond with block and sashing placement in adjoining rows.

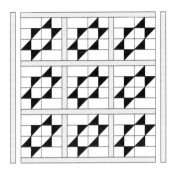

6. Cut and sew two long vertical sashing strips to the sides of the quilt. To calculate length, figure the lengths of components in the same manner as for horizontal pieces. Be sure to add ½" (1.2 cm) to the figure to allow for seams on each end. fig. 8

Additional Settings

Keep layout options in mind as you design your quilt. Look at as many quilting books as you can. Visit quilt shows to see contemporary pieces and browse antique shops to view vintage quilts. Think of the diagrams in this chapter only as a starting point, and then use our size charts and your own creativity to step in and make changes. You'll end up with a quilt that is truly your own design.

Working with Borders

Think of borders as a frame for a painting. The type of framing you choose can dramatically change the final look of any piece. They are particularly important for small and miniature quilts that will be used in a decorative way. Borders also act as anchors for the quilt and can help you square up a slightly skewed piece.

Types of Borders

Borders can be *straight sewn* or *mitered*. They can be simply or intricately pieced. Blocks or squares can be inserted at their corners. They can be scalloped all the way around or rounded only at the corners. Borders do not have to be identical on all sides. *Blazing Baskets* on page 3 has an inner border on the top and bottom of the quilt only, with a wider border around all sides. If the inner border were omitted, the quilt would be square rather than rectangular.

Not all of the patterns in this book include borders, but you have the option of adding them if you wish. For quilts that do have borders, we provide recommended widths. You might prefer to alter those widths to suit your needs. For small quilts, fabric requirements are based on crosswise strips if it provides enough length to cut each border without piecing. Fabric charts for larger quilts assume you will cut borders on the lengthwise grain to avoid piecing. You must usually purchase extra fabric for mitered borders. If you need to add stability to a stretchy quilt, use lengthwise grain strips, which have less give than crosswise strips.

Do not cut border strips until your quilt top is finished because actual dimensions of a finished quilt are usually not the same for everyone.

Making Straight-Sewn Borders

1. To determine side border length, measure the quilt top from top to bottom through its vertical midpoint. Measuring along quilt edges is usually not accurate, because they are often stretched out of shape a little.

2. Cut two side borders to exactly match the length determined in Step 1. Fold a border in half crosswise and crease to determine its

midpoint. Pin the midpoint to the horizontal midpoint of the quilt, matching edges with right sides together. Match and pin at the ends, and then continue pinning along the entire length of both pieces. Manipulate fabrics with your fingers and pin at close intervals to ease in fullness if necessary.

3. Sew the border to the quilt with a ¼" (0.6 cm) seam allowance. If you had to ease in fullness, sew with the longer piece next to the feed dogs. Add the border to the opposite side in the same way. Press seam allowances toward the borders.

4. To determine top and bottom border length, measure the quilt top from side to side through its horizontal midpoint, including the side borders. Cut two borders that length.

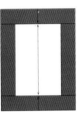

5. Fold a border in half crosswise and crease to determine its midpoint. Right sides together, pin the midpoint to the vertical midpoint on one side of the quilt, and then pin at each end, matching raw edges as for side borders. Ease in fullness if necessary. Sew together with a ¼" (0.6 cm) seam allowance. Repeat to add border on the opposite end. Press seam allowances toward the borders.

6. Use Steps 1 to 5 to measure and add additional borders to the quilt.

Making Mitered Borders

Mitered borders can be used any time, but they are a good choice for directional fabrics, such as stripes, which look best if matched at corners so that the design flows in a continuous stream around the quilt. Special border prints are perfect candidates for mitering. When mirror images are sewn together at each corner, they create a kaleidoscope design which can enhance the beauty of your quilt.

1. Measure the quilt through its vertical and horizontal midpoints. To each of those figures, add 2 times the finished width of the border, plus 4" (10 cm). Cut two borders each length.

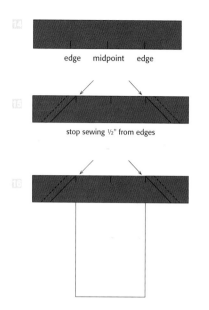

edge   midpoint   edge

stop sewing ½" from edges

2. Fold a border crosswise to find its midpoint. On the edge that will be aligned for sewing, mark the midpoint with a pin, and then measure outward along the border to pin mark the ending length of the quilt on each side. Use the quilt measurement determined in Step 1. Do not match it to the side of the quilt to determine length. Repeat with remaining borders.

3. Beginning exactly at a marked end point, align a ruler to draw a 45° diagonal line to represent the finished seam line where borders will be joined at corners. Mark a second line parallel to and ¼" (0.6 cm) past the first. This is the cutting line, but do not cut until borders are sewn to the quilt. Repeat on the opposite end of strip and on remaining borders. Draw miters in the correct direction.

4. Align a border to the quilt as for straight-sewn borders, pinning midpoints and ends first and then pinning along an entire side.

5. Sew the border to the quilt with a ¼" (0.6 cm) seam allowance. Backstitch at stop and start points. Using pin marks as a guide, avoid sewing into seam allowance at either end.

6. Repeat Steps 4 and 5 to sew remaining borders to the quilt.

7. Fold quilt corners diagonally, right sides together. Match and pin the marked sewing lines at one corner. End points of adjacent seams should match. Begin sewing at the same spot where previous seams ended. Backstitch at the beginning of the seam and continue sewing to the ends of strips. Trim marked cutting line and press seam open. Repeat on remaining corners.

Making Borders with Corner Blocks or Squares

1. Measure the quilt top vertically and horizontally as for straight-sewn borders. Cut two border strips for each length.

2. If more than one border will surround the corner block, cut remaining borders the same lengths and sew strips side by side to add as one unit.

3. Sew side borders to the quilt, aligning as described for straight-sewn borders. Press seam allowances toward the borders.

4. Cut or piece corner squares equal to the finished width of the border, plus a total of ½" (1.2 cm) for the seam allowance. Sew a corner square to each end of the top and bottom borders. Press seam allowances toward the borders.

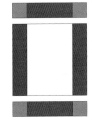

5. Sew top and bottom borders to the quilt, matching midpoints, ends, and seam intersections first and then matching edges along the entire side of each. Press seam allowances toward the borders.

Making Pieced Borders

Borders can be pieced as simply or intricately as you desire. Be sure to plan their layout to work mathematically with both sides of the quilt. For instance, it would be difficult to align 3" × 3" (7.5 cm × 7.5 cm) units to both sides of a quilt that finishes at 18" × 26" (45 cm × 65 cm). Three divides equally into 18, but not 26. If you cannot find a common denominator, adding borders often helps. For instance, 2" (5 cm) added to each of the previous dimensions would result in a quilt 20" × 28", which would allow you to use 4" (10 cm) units in the border. Another option is to place narrow strips between pieced units, which alters the number required on each side.

Multiple Borders

If you are using more than one mitered border, sew all strips together lengthwise for each side, and then add to the quilt as a unit, matching strips when you sew the miters. For easier matching, press seam allowances in side borders in the opposite direction as seam allowances in top and bottom borders.

Catching the View

CHAPTER 10

Assembling and Finishing

When your quilt top is assembled, it is time to mark it for quilting and to make the "quilt sandwich" by layering the top with batting and backing. The final steps of quilting and binding are exciting ones, because everything you have worked to achieve comes together to create a quilt you will be proud to display. It is the quilting design and quilting stitches that separate your quilt from ordinary bedcovers. Take the time to finish the quilt as carefully as you began.

Marking Quilting Motifs

An easy way to mark quilting designs is to trace through stencils. Designs are available commercially, or you can trace your own on template plastic and cut out the design with a double-bladed craft knife or stencil burner. If you use a lead pencil, choose a #3 or #4, keep it sharp, and mark very lightly. Other choices are Berol Verithin pencils, available in many colors. Marks are made before the quilt top is sandwiched with batting and backing. To avoid heat-setting lines, be sure to press the quilt before it is marked.

If you plan to outline quilt in ¼″ (0.6 cm) increments away from shapes, you may not need to mark at all. Judge the distance as you work, or apply ¼″ (0.6 cm) masking tape as a guide. When one area is finished, move the tape to the next section to be quilted. Other straight lines can be marked using your rotary rulers as a guide.

If you plan to machine-quilt, try a tear-away product. Quilting designs are printed on paper, which is pinned to the sandwiched quilt. After quilting, the paper is removed.

Quilting guides can be made from freezer paper. Cut out a shape and press it to the sandwiched quilt top. Quilt around it, and then pull it away and quilt in another area.

Backing

Do not skimp on the quality of backing fabric. Do not spend time piecing a gorgeous quilt and then use backing that bleeds every time it gets damp.

Backings can be assembled in any configuration you desire. We try to cut and sew pieces to make best use of the available fabric, but you may choose to make a more decorative backing, or even a reversible quilt.

Seams can run horizontally or vertically, but try to configure pieced backings so that seams do not fall on the quilt's midpoints.

Make a quilt back that is 2″ × 4″ (5 cm to 10 cm) wider than the quilt on all sides. Many of the quilts in this book are small, so backings

can be cut from a single width of fabric. Standard 44″-wide (110 cm) fabric must be pieced to back quilts with sides longer than 40″ (100 cm).

1. Measure the quilt horizontally and vertically. Cut a single piece of backing 2″ to 3″ (5 cm to 7.5 cm) wider and longer than the quilt. If backing must be pieced, decide how many panels you will use and if seams will be horizontal or vertical.

2. Remove selvages from fabric. Determine strip widths required to piece the configuration you have chosen. Add ¼″ (0.6 cm) to outer panels, and ½″ (1.2 cm) to an inner panel that will be joined on both sides. Sew panels together lengthwise.

3. Press seam allowances open, especially if you intend to hand-quilt. Pressing to the side is usually the best choice to stabilize seams in bed quilts that will be washed often and receive nightly use, but these little quilts won't be under that kind of stress.

Batting for Small Quilts

Overall, quilt battings are divided into two categories, natural and synthetic. Wool, cotton, and silk are all natural fibers; polyester is synthetic. We suggest you visit local quilt shops and read labels to learn more about batting characteristics and care. Some shops and mail order sources offer batting-swatch samples which help you make comparisons.

Most quilts in this book contain either wool or low-loft (thin) cotton batting. In a few cases, batting was divided into layers to make it thinner. Wool drapes nicely and is easy to hand- or machine-quilt. One hundred percent cotton batting is usually more difficult to hand-quilt but easy to quilt by machine. Some batting products labeled as cotton are actually blends of 80 percent cotton and 20 percent polyester. They provide easier needling for hand-quilters and do not need to be as closely quilted as pure cotton batts.

Polyester batts are easy to hand-quilt, but avoid those that are high-loft (thick). Their fluffy appearance is not usually suitable for wall quilts. Polyester batts tend to beard, meaning that fibers can migrate onto the top and backing of your quilt. Bearding can be diminished if quilting is done at closer intervals. Perhaps the most important thing to say about polyester is that it melts at high temperatures. Avoid using a polyester batt in any quilt that will be near a heat source.

Batting for Miniature and Wall Quilts

Batting	Content	Characteristics
Fairfield Cotton Classic	80% cotton 20% polyester	Flat, antique look
Flannel (various sources)	100% cotton	Thin, flat
Hobbs Heirloom Cotton	80% cotton 20% polyester	Flat, antique look
Hobbs Thermore	100% polyester	Thin, flat
Hobbs wool	100% wool	Low loft
Mountain Mist Blue Ribbon	100% cotton	Flat, antique look
Silk (various sources)	100% silk	Very thin, excellent for dollhouse or miniatures
Warm & Natural	100% cotton needle-punched into polyester base	Flat, dense, easy to hand-quilt

Making the Quilt Sandwich

1. Place the backing right side down on a smooth, flat surface. For small quilts, use masking tape to hold down the edges, pulling the backing taut without stretching it out of shape.

2. Preshrink batting if necessary, taking care to follow the manufacturer's instructions. Center the batting on top of the backing, smoothing out any creases. If creases persist, allow the batting to rest for awhile, or tumble it in a cool clothes dryer for a few minutes.

3. Trim stray threads on the quilt top. Center the pressed top right side up on top of the batting, smoothing any wrinkles. Make sure backing and batting extend past the quilt's edges by 2″ to 4″ (5 cm to 10 cm).

4. Thread- or pin-baste to secure the layers. If you thread-baste, use a darning needle and a white or neutral thread. Use enough basting stitches so that layers will remain stable as the quilt is handled. Use safety pins that will not rust, and minimize hole size by using as small a pin as you can comfortably place through layers. We like to use tiny brass safety pins for very small quilts with thin batting. Tacking tools are another basting option.

5. Remove masking tape and quilt the piece.

Hand Quilting

Needles

Hand quilting is accomplished using short, sturdy needles called *betweens*. Hand-sewing needles decrease in size as their numerical designations increase. For instance, a #12 needle is smaller than a #10. Small needles generally produce smaller stitches, but select a size you feel comfortable working with. Fine-wired needle threaders are almost essential to easily thread a number #12 needle.

Thread

Hand quilting thread is stronger than all-purpose sewing thread. If you must quilt with all-purpose thread, strengthen it by coating lengths with beeswax, available in most fabric shops. Knot the end of thread that came off the spool last. One hundred percent cotton thread is usually recommended for bed quilts, to keep thread content compatible with fabric content. But for wallhangings, you might prefer a more decorative look. Try using metallic threads, or any other bright thread.

Quilting Frames

Lap hoops or rectangular frames are suitable for small quilts. If the quilt is small, pinning a piece of flannel or terrycloth to one side before inserting in a round hoop will keep it taut and prevent stretching.

Thimbles

Thimbles are used on top of the quilt to push the needle down through layers. The tip of the finger used to feel the needle underneath will callous over time from repeated pin-pricking. You can avoid needle sticks and callouses by shielding that finger with a few layers of masking tape or selecting a finger guard from a growing number of commercial products.

The Quilting Stitch

1. Thread a needle with approximately 18″ (45 cm) of thread. Knot the end by wrapping the thread's tail around the needle a few times. Pull needle through the wraps, holding them with your fingers. Keep pulling until the wrapped threads are at the end of the strand.

2. Insert the needle through the quilt top approximately 1″ (2.5 cm) from where you plan to start quilting. Do not go through to the backing. Bring the needle back up directly on a quilting line and tug the thread to pop the knot into the batting.

3. Position the needle so that it is perpendicular to the quilt's surface. Let it move downward, but do not push it with the thimble. When you feel the tip of the needle on the underneath side, push it upward toward the top of the quilt. Move it downward again to take another stitch. With this rocking motion, several stitches can be loaded on the needle before it is pushed to the surface and pulled through.

4. To end a line of stitching, bring the needle up through the fabric just past the final stitch. Make a loop as the last length of thread comes through the top, and use your fingers to form a knot about ¼" (0.6 cm) away from the quilt top. Insert the needle into the quilt top, directly where thread is coming out. Bring the needle back through the quilt top about 1" (2.5 cm) away, tugging to pop the thread into the batting. Cut the thread flush with the quilt top. Begin quilting where the last stitch ended or in a new area.

Do not be too concerned if your stitches are long; they will shorten with practice.

Machine Quilting

Straight-line machine quilting is best accomplished with a walking foot, also called an even-feed foot. This specialized presser foot grips the top of the quilt to advance it through the machine at the same rate as the backing, which is moved along by the feed dogs. It helps to keep the layers from tugging apart as they are sewn, reducing distortion and pleats on the front and back of the quilt. Gentle curves are possible with the walking foot, but reserve intricate patterns for free-motion techniques.

Free-motion machine-quilting is done with a darning foot, or a similar specialized foot with a larger opening. Feed dogs are placed in the down position. The quilter controls stitch length by needle speed and the rate at which the quilt is moved under the needle. Stitches can be random or follow a marked line. Free-motion quilting takes practice, but once you've mastered it there's no limit to the designs you can achieve.

Threads

Machine quilters often use very fine nylon thread through the needle. The indentations of stitches are visible, but the thread itself is more diffi-cult to see, which helps make the piece look a bit more like traditional hand quilting. Clear nylon is best for light fabrics, smoke for darker fabrics. A large variety of decorative threads are also available. Light-weight threads, such as those used for lingerie, are used in the bobbin.

Top and/or bottom needle tension must usually be adjusted for both kinds of machine-quilting.

Binding

Binding encompasses the raw edges of the quilt sandwich. It can blend or contrast with the quilt or borders. You can repeat a fabric used within the quilt or select an entirely new one. The finished width of binding depends on the type of quilt you are making and how the quilt will be used.

Mitered Binding

1. When you've finished quilting, use your rotary equipment to trim the batting and backing to match the quilt top, squaring up corners if necessary. Be sure to leave a ¼″ (0.6 cm) seam allowance around the outer perimeter of the quilt.

2. Measure the quilt vertically and horizontally and multiply the measurement by 2. Add 12″ (25 cm) to that figure. This is the length you must make binding.

3. Determine the width of binding. For most quilts, a doublefold binding provides the nicest edge. Avoid using heavy fabrics on small quilts. Crosswise grain strips are less stretchy to work with than bias strips. The width of your cut strips depends on the finished width of the binding and the amount of loft in the batting. For ¼″ (0.6 cm) finished binding, use strips 2″ to 2¾″ (5 cm to 6.9 cm) wide.

4. When you must join strips to achieve the required length, place them right sides together and perpendicular to each other. Mark the top strip on the diagonal and then sew a seam on the line. Cut off the excess fabric, leaving a ¼″ (0.6 cm) seam allowance. Press the seam open and trim nubs made by seam allowance. Join additional strips until binding is the correct length. fig. 2

5. Press the binding along the lengthwise midpoint of the strip. For instance, a 2"-wide (5 cm) strip will become a 1" (2.5 cm) strip with a fold along one edge.

6. Align the raw edges of the binding with an edge on the front side of the quilt. Do not start in a corner. Pin the binding along the side, leaving a 3"-long (7.5 cm) tail loose at the beginning. Align binding to the rest of the quilt, without pinning, to make sure strip intersections will not end up in a corner, where they will create too much bulk. If they do, shift the start point to another area.

7. Sew the binding to the quilt using the predetermined seam width. Stop sewing before you reach the corner, ending your seam the same distance from the edge as the width of the seam allowance. End the seam ¼" (0.6 cm) from the corner if you are sewing a ¼" (0.6 cm) seam. Backstitch and remove the quilt from the machine.

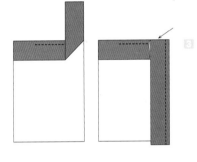

8. Fold the long end of the binding straight up, over the seam you just sewed, positioning it so that it is parallel to the next side of the quilt. There will be a 45° angle on the strip's lower right edge. Fold the binding down again, the fold flush with the top of the quilt and raw edges aligned with the sides. The angle should still be intact underneath the folded edge, and all sides should meet. fig. 3

9. Pin the binding to the next side and continue sewing, beginning where the previous seam ended. Backstitch at the start of the seam.

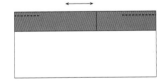

10. When you near the next corner, stop and backstitch. Miter the corner as before and continue sewing along the next side. Treat each corner in the same way.

11. Stop sewing 4" to 6" (10 cm to 15 cm) from the starting point or just past the last corner. Backstitch. For small quilts this means a wide section of the last edge may be unsewn. Trim end of tail, leaving it long enough to overlap the unsewn tail at the start by about 4" (10 cm). fig. 4

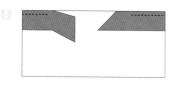

Singlefold Binding

A single thickness of binding can be sewn to the quilt and then folded under in back before it is sewn in place.

Binding Alternative

Some quilters like to apply binding before the edges of the quilt are trimmed. Try both methods to see which you like best.

12. Beginning at the raw edge, make a 45° cut in the starting tail.

13. Lay the ending tail under the angled starting tail. Draw a line next to and matching the diagonal cut. Add a ½″ (1.2 cm) seam allowance to the diagonal edge of the ending tail and trim.

14. Place the angled tails right sides together, offsetting ends by ¼″ (0.6 cm). Sew together with a ¼″ (0.6 cm) seam allowance.

15. Binding length should now match the unsewn edge. Pin it to the quilt and sew to complete the binding.

16. Beginning on one side, take the folded edge of binding to the back of the quilt. It should fit snugly over the quilt's edge. Hold in place with pins, or use binding clips. Miters will form automatically at front corners, and will be easily created with folds on the quilt back. Use a blindstitch and matching thread to sew the binding to the quilt back, taking a few stitches in each rear miter to hold it in place.

Self-Binding

To make a self-binding, sometimes called a rolled binding, select a fabric backing that complements the quilt. Move the backing out of the way and trim edges of batting to match quilt, squaring up corners if necessary. Trim the backing so that it extends ¾″ to 1″ (1.9 cm to 2.5 cm) past the quilt on all sides. Fold under to create a finished edge, and blindstitch the fold to the quilt front. Miter corners as you come to them, trimming excess fabric that will lie under the fold if necessary.

Straight Binding

Use four single-fold strips of fabric, applying each to the quilt independently. Sew binding to two opposite sides first, and then fold edges under and blindstitch to the back. Trim flush with quilt sides. Sew the two remaining strips to the quilt. Blindstitch to the back, turning under raw edges at ends and overlapping first bindings on each side. Double-fold binding is not recommended for this method. It creates too much bulk at overlapped ends.

Hanging the Quilt

1. Cut a 9"-wide (22.5 cm) piece of fabric about 2" (5 cm) shorter than the width of the quilt.

2. Turn under each end by ½" (1.2 cm). Press. Sew a straight or zigzag seam to secure ends.

3. Place wrong sides of the strip together, aligning raw edges. Sew lengthwise with a ½" (1.2 cm) seam allowance. Press the seam open and center it on the back of the tube.

4. Center the tube near the top edge of the quilt, seam against the backing. Use a blindstitch to sew the tube to the quilt around its top and bottom edges and sides.

   Use a decorative curtain rod or dowel or a commercial quilt hanger to mount the quilt on the wall.

Wide Binding

If your quilt does not have borders, the final seam around its perimeter will probably need to be sewn ¼" (.6 cm) inward from all sides. Sewing a wider seam will result in inaccurate patches around the outside edges of the quilt. To add a wide binding, square up the quilt top, folding the batting and backing out of the way before trimming each side. Deduct ¼" (.6 cm) from the desired finished width of the binding, and trim the batting and backing to extend past all edges of the quilt by that width. Calculate required strip width and sew the binding to the quilt.

Narrow Bindings

If you plan to sew a ¼" (0.6 cm) binding seam, then trim it back to a narrower width. Make the folds at each corner based on the final width of the binding. For instance, for a binding you will trim back to ⅛" (0.3 cm), begin each fold ⅛" (0.3 cm) inward from the quilt's edge rather than folding the binding so that it is flush with the quilt. Larger folds create too much bulk at miters.

Sleeve Option

If you like, the raw edges of a folded tube can be sewn to the quilt top when binding is applied.

Half Log Cabin dollhouse miniature

CHAPTER 11

Additional Techniques

There may be times when you wish to use a block from a pattern but in a different size than the pattern provides. Analyzing the individual units within a block will help you draft them quickly and easily. In this chapter, we will explain how to scale up or scale down any pattern to suit your needs. We will also cover the tiniest miniatures of all—dollhouse quilts.

Reducing and Enlarging Blocks

If you plan to use templates to assemble blocks, the individual units within them can be any size, because the templates provide you with exact marking and cutting guides. However, if you wish to use rotary-cutting techniques, the smallest units in your blocks should be in increments of no less than $\frac{1}{8}''$ (0.3 cm), which is the smallest measurement marked on most rotary rulers.

Blocks are generally referred to as One-Patch, Four-Patch, Five-Patch, Seven-Patch, and Nine-Patch. The designations refer to the number of equal divisions across the width of each block type. Grids can be divided again equally to create more squares or combined equally to create fewer squares.

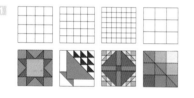
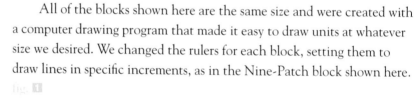

All of the blocks shown here are the same size and were created with a computer drawing program that made it easy to draw units at whatever size we desired. We changed the rulers for each block, setting them to draw lines in specific increments, as in the Nine-Patch block shown here. fig. **1**

It would be difficult to rotary-cut all four blocks to finish at the same size, because we cannot change the markings on our rotary rulers. Pieces for the Five-Patch block would be easy to cut for a block that finishes at $5'' \times 5''$ or $10'' \times 10''$ (12.5 cm $\times$ 12.5 cm or 25 cm $\times$ 25 cm), because both sizes are divisible by 5, the number of grids across and down. The Nine-Patch block could not be rotary-cut to finish at those sizes, because units would be a fractional dimension that is not marked on rulers.

If you wish to combine block types in a quilt, you must find a common denominator for each. For instance, both Four-Patch and Nine-Patch blocks can be rotary-cut to finish at $12'' \times 12''$ (30 cm $\times$ 30 cm), because units required for both will divide equally into that number.

When you must choose a size, look at blocks from a units perspective. If you wish your Five-Patch block to finish in the range of $6'' \times 6''$ (15 cm $\times$ 15 cm), divide 6 (15 cm) by 5. The answer, 1.2″, is not a dimension that can be cut with rotary equipment, but rounding it up to

1.25 or 1¼″ (3.1 cm) will work fine. Using 1¼″ (3.1 cm) units will result in a block that finishes at 6¼″ × 6¼″ (15 cm × 15 cm), not a drastic size increase.

If your quilt must finish at a specific size, adjust dimensions by altering the width of sashing or borders. If your blocks must be a size that cannot be rotary-cut, draw the block on drafting paper and make templates to mark and cut each piece (see page 140).

An Introduction to Dollhouse Miniatures

A dollhouse miniature is a quilt made to a very small scale, usually to fit on a doll's bed. A scale of 1 to 12 is the most popular size. That is, if a typical double bed quilt measures 84″ × 96″ (210 cm × 240 cm), a dollhouse version of the same quilt would measure 7″ × 8″ (17.5 cm × 20 cm). Quite simply a typical 12″-square (30 cm) block is reduced to 1″ × 1″ (2.5 cm × 2.5 cm), or a typical 15″-square (37.5 cm) block is reduced to 1¼″ × 1¼″ (3.1 cm × 3.1 cm).

Both of the dollhouse miniatures in this book, *Little Amish Squares* on page 56 and *Half Log Cabin* on page 62, are sewn with 1″ × 1″ (2.5 cm × 2.5 cm) blocks, but do not let the tiny patch size discourage you. The blocks are foundation pieced, which means you will not handle little bits of fabric. Every block will be perfect if you position fabric carefully and sew directly on marked template lines. Turn to page 131 for more information about foundation piecing.

Layout Options

Dollhouse quilts sometimes drape over miniature beds more attractively if blocks are omitted from bottom corners. This allows the end of the quilt to be tucked between the mattress and the footboard and leaves the sides free to fall straight toward the floor.

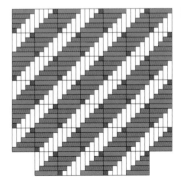

Batting and Binding

Sometimes it's best to omit batting in these little quilts, particularly those with many closely spaced seams, which tend to stiffen the top. The quilt's ability to drape is important and disappears if you add too much depth. You do not want to end up with something that resembles a potholder more than it does a bedcover. Try silk batting or tear away a very thin layer from a cotton batt.

As with larger quilts, binding can be applied separately, or it can be created by folding the backing's raw edge under and stitching it to the front of the quilt. Avoid using double-fold bindings. They are usually too bulky for tiny quilts.

Draping the Quilt

If the quilt is stiff, try one of these methods to help it drape over the bed.

- Insert a length of fine-gauge wire along each lengthwise edge or other areas where shaping must take place. Bend wire to mold the quilt to the desired shape.

- Dampen the quilt and mold it to the shape of the bed. Be sure to use prewashed fabrics that will not bleed.

If you do not wish to use the 1″ × 1″ (2.5 cm × 2.5 cm) blocks to make a dollhouse quilt, try sewing them in pieced borders or sashing or in clusters as embellishments for clothing. Use them to make quilts for larger-scale doll furniture or in any other way you desire. You will find many ways to use these versatile little blocks.

Templates

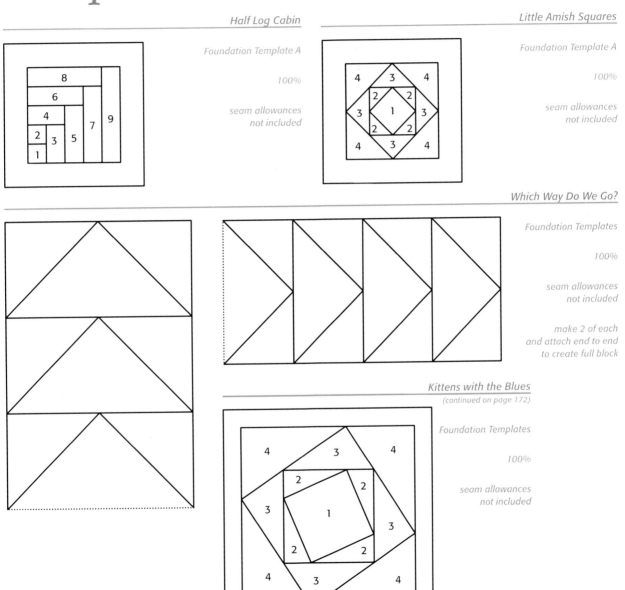

Foundation Template A

100%

seam allowances
not included

8
6
4
7   9
2   3   5
1

Foundation Template A

100%

seam allowances
not included

4   3   4
2   2
3   1   3
2   2
4   3   4

Foundation Templates

100%

seam allowances
not included

make 2 of each
and attach end to end
to create full block

(continued on page 172)

Foundation Templates

100%

seam allowances
not included

4   3   4
2   2
3   1
2   2   3
4   3   4

Foundation Templates

100%

seam allowances included

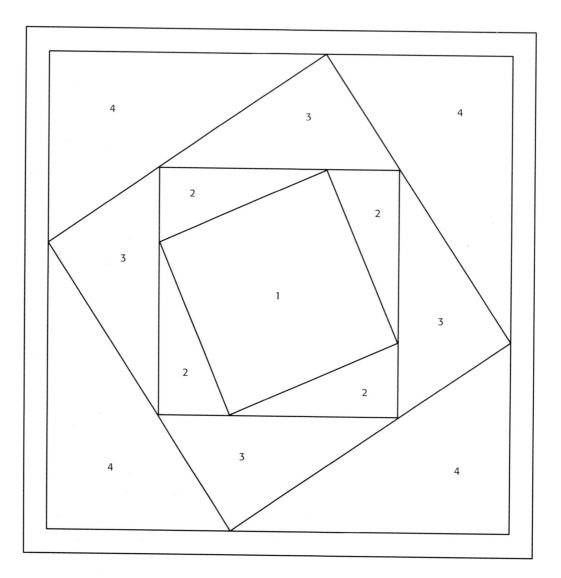

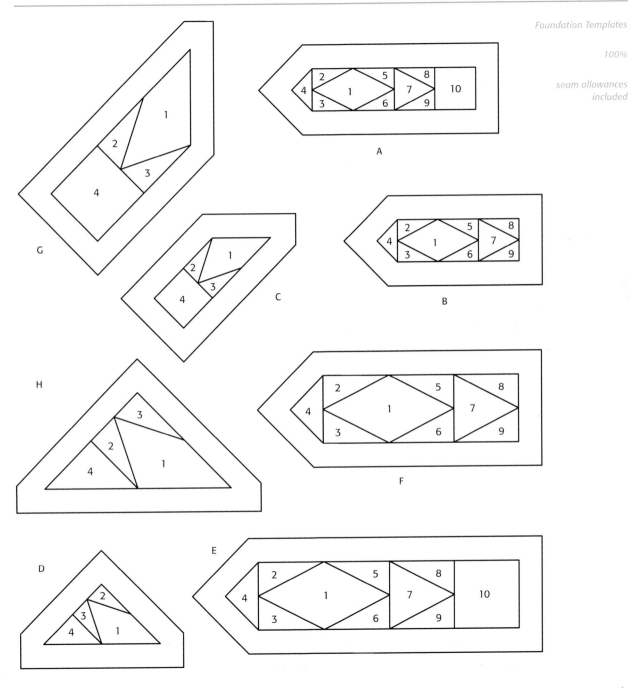

100%

C, F include seam allowances

A, B do not include
seam allowances

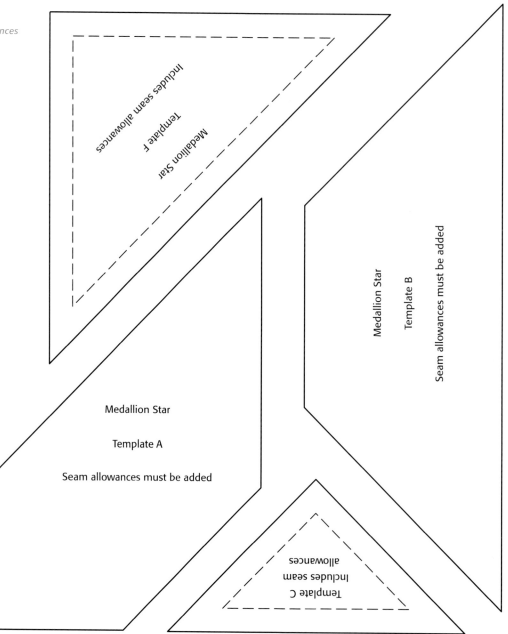

Medallion Star

Template F

Includes seam allowances

Medallion Star

Template B

Seam allowances must be added

Medallion Star

Template A

Seam allowances must be added

Template C

Includes seam
allowances

(continued on page 175)

100%

*D does not include
seam allowances*

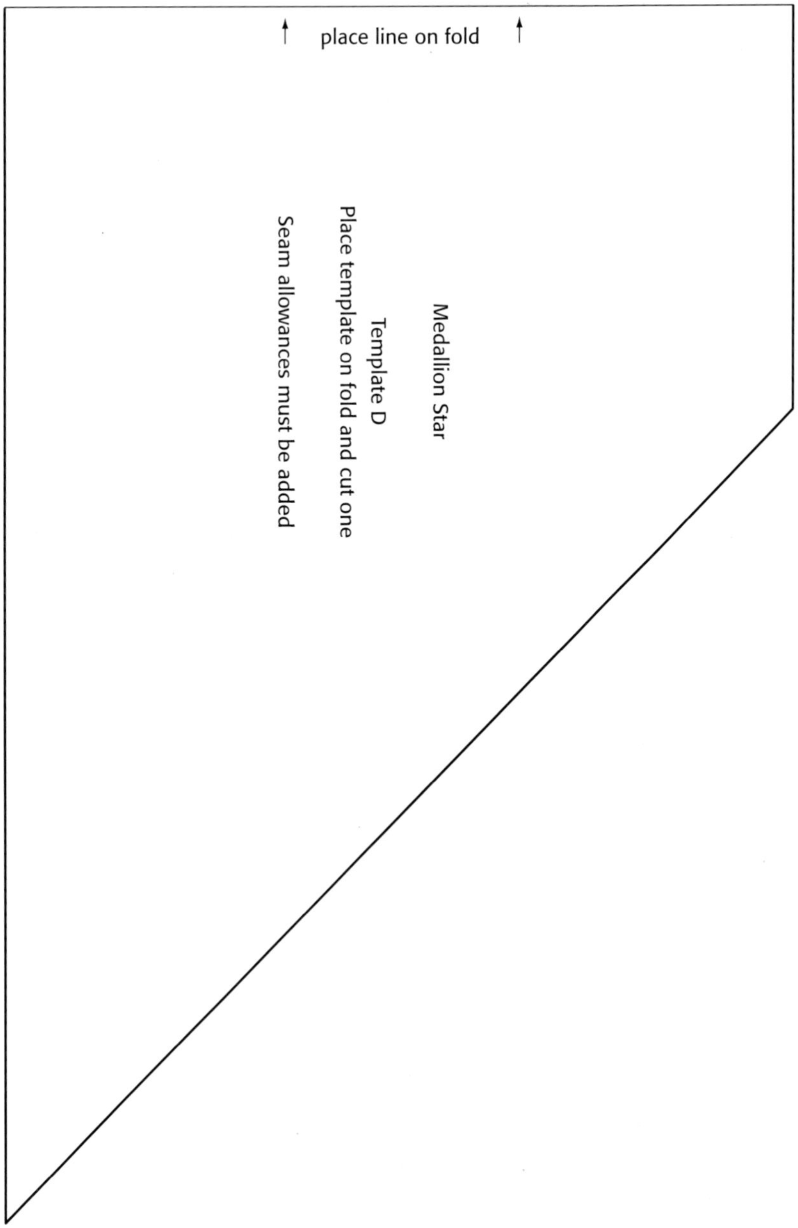

place line on fold

Medallion Star

Template D
Place template on fold and cut one

Seam allowances must be added

100%

E does not include seam allowances

*Join template halves
at dotted line,
matching points a and b*

a

b

Medallion Star

½ of Template E
Join template halves at dotted line,
matching points a and b

Seam allowances must be added

Medallion Star

½ of Template E
Join template halves at dotted line,
matching points a and b

Seam allowances must be added

a

b

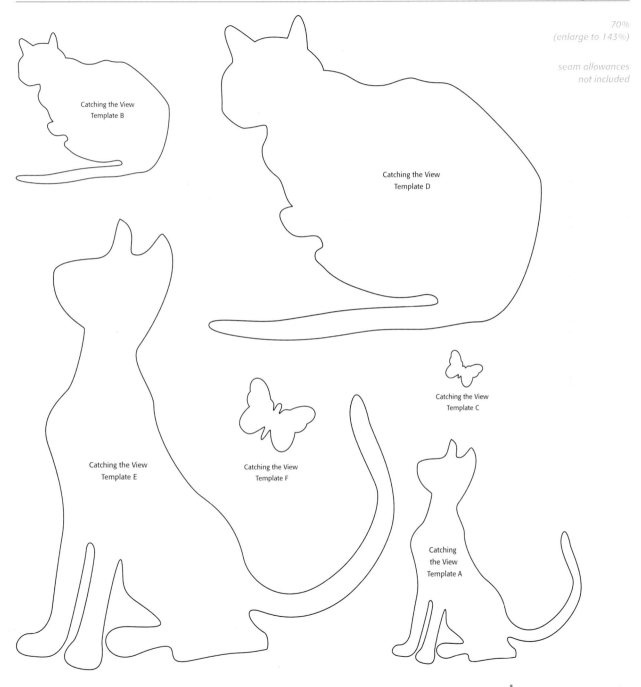

Catching the View
Template B

Catching the View
Template D

Catching the View
Template E

Catching the View
Template F

Catching the View
Template C

Catching
the View
Template A

(continued on page 179)

*Foundation Templates !00%
seam allowances included*

*Appliqué Templates 75%
enlarge to 133%
seam allowances
not included*

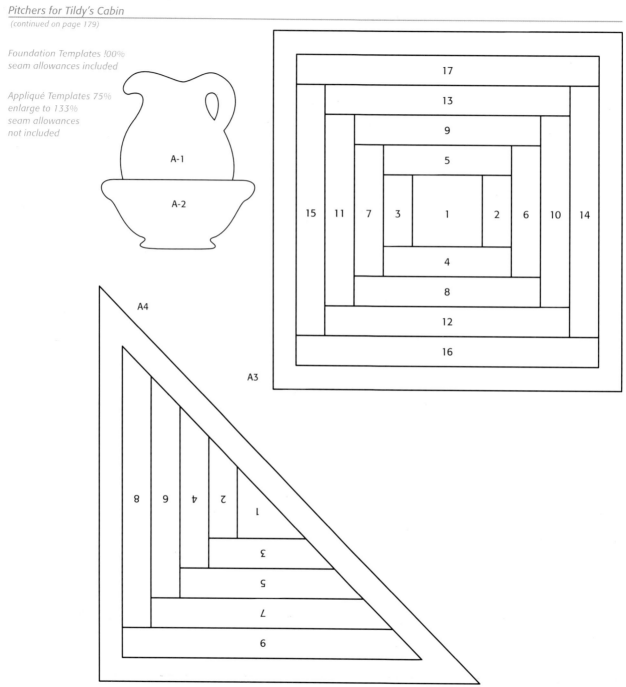

A-1

A-2

17

13

9

5

15 11 7 3 1 2 6 10 14

4

8

12

16

A3

A4

8 6 4 2 1

3

5

7

9

(continued on page 180)

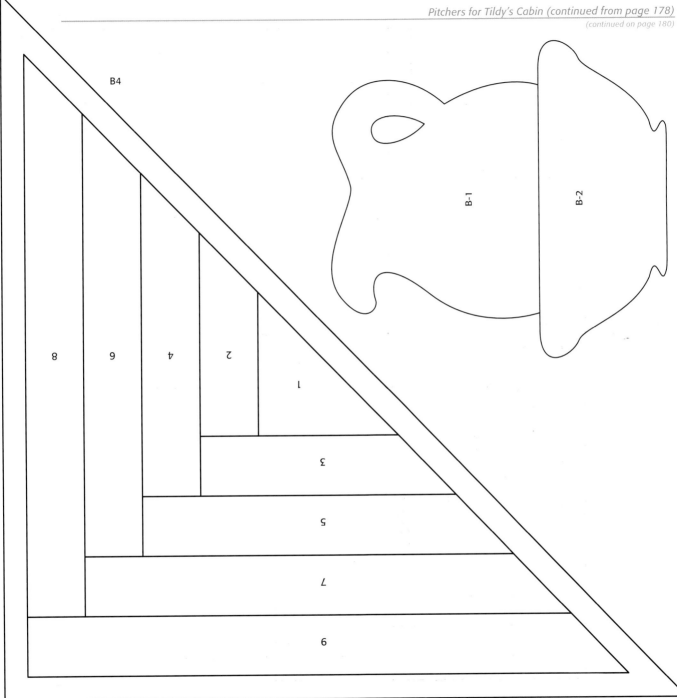

B4

B-1

B-2

8

6

4

2

1

3

5

7

9

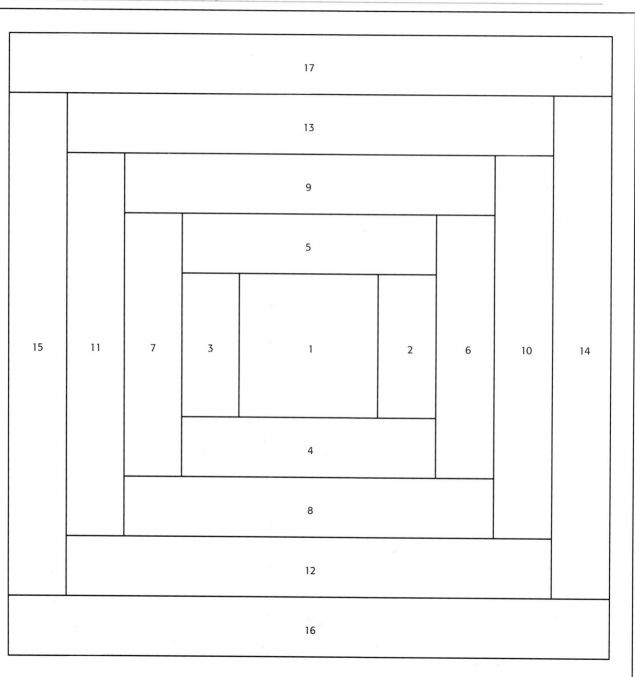

Glossary

B

Betweens
Short, sturdy needles used for the quilting stitch.

Bias
A 45° angle to the straight grain in a piece of fabric.

Binding
A long narrow strip of cloth that folds over and holds together the raw edges of a quilt.

Bleeding
Occurs when dye is lost from a fabric.

C

Chain piecing
Assembly-line piecing, where aligned units are fed through the sewing machine one after another without breaking the threads between them.

Concave curve
A curve that rounds inward.

Convex curve
A curve that rounds outward.

E

Easing
Pinning and using your fingers to adjust adjoining units of uneven lengths so they match for sewing.

F

Fat eighth
A ⅛ yard cut of fabric that measures 9″ × 22″ (23 cm × 56 cm).

Fat quarter
A ¼ yard cut of fabric that measures 18″ × 22″ (46 cm × 56 cm).

Foundation template
An exact copy of a block or portion of a block. Fabric is sewn directly to the template.

A

Appliqué
Sewing small pieces of fabric to a larger background.

B

Backing
The fabric panel used as the back piece of a layered quilt.

Backstitch
Stitching backwards over previous stitches to strengthen seams. In quilting, most often done during setting-in.

Basting
Securing two or more fabric layers together with long stitches or safety pins in preparation for final sewing.

Batting
The material used as a stuffing between the quilt top and backing.

Bearding
Occurs when batting fibers migrate through the quilt top or back.

L

Loft
The thickness of batting. Low-loft batting is most useful for small quilts.

M

Matchwork
Random quilting stitches that move across the quilt. They generally do not overlap.

P

Patchwork
Small pieces of fabric that are sewn together to form a larger piece. The act of sewing them together is called piecing.

Pressing
Setting an iron up and down on top of units to press seams and remove wrinkles.

Q

Quick-piecing
Sewing fabric together using techniques that eliminate the handling of individual patches.

S

Sashing
Plain or pieced strips that are sewn between blocks.

Seam allowance
The width between the seam line and the outer edge of patches. We normally use a 1/40 (0.6 cm) seam allowance.

Selvage
The outer, finished edges of fabric that run parallel to the lengthwise grain.

Setting
The way elements of a quilt are sewn together.

Setting-in
Sewing a patch into an opening created by previously joined patches.

Setting square
A plain square of fabric sewn between pieced or appliquéd blocks.

Setting triangle
A triangle used to fill in the jagged edges left around the outer perimeter of a quilt where blocks are placed on-point.

Sharps
Long, thin needles used for appliqué and other hand sewing.

Stipple quilting
Closely spaced, random quilting stitches that tend to flatten the quilted area. Often used around appliqué motifs.

Straight set
A setting in which blocks are placed so that their straight sides are parallel to the sides of the quilt.

Strip piecing
A quick-piecing technique where long strips of fabric are joined lengthwise into strip sets to mimic a portion of a block. Short segments are cut from the set and then sewn with other segments to form the desired layouts.

T

Template
A rigid, exact copy of a pattern piece.

W

Walking foot
Also called an even-feed foot. A sewing machine presser foot with an advancing mechanism that works with feed dogs to advance both layers of a unit at the same rate.

Warp threads
The long threads secured to ends of a loom during the weaving process. They become the lengthwise grain.

Weft threads
The threads that are woven across the warp threads. They become the crosswise grain.